Integrated Korean
Beginning 1

KLEAR Textbooks in Korean Language

Integrated Korean

Beginning 1

Second Edition

Young-mee Cho   Hyo Sang Lee   Carol Schulz   Ho-min Sohn   Sung-Ock Sohn

University of Hawai'i Press
Honolulu

© 2010 University of Hawai'i Press
All rights reserved
Printed in the United States of America
23 22 21 20 19   11 10 9 8 7

This textbook series has been developed by the Korean Language Education and Research Center (KLEAR) with the support of the Korea Foundation.

Library of Congress Cataloging-in-Publication Data
Integrated Korean : beginning / Young-mee Cho ... [et al.].—2nd ed.
    p.   cm.—(KLEAR textbooks in Korean language)
  English and Korean.
  ISBN 978-0-8248-3440-1 (v. 1 : alk. paper)
  1. Korean language—Textbooks for foreign speakers—English.   I. Cho, Young-mee.
II. Series.
  PL913.I5812 2009
495.7′82421—dc22

                                        2009075350

Illustrations and photos by Sejin Han

Audio files for this volume may be downloaded on the web in RealAudio or MP3 format at http://www.kleartextbook.com

A set of accompanying audio CDs for this book is also available for purchase. For more information, contact:

Order Department
University of Hawai'i Press
2840 Kolowalu Street
Honolulu, Hawaii 96822
Toll free: 888-847-7377
Outside North America: 808-956-8255

Camera-ready copy has been provided by the authors.

University of Hawai'i Press books are printed on acid-free paper and meet the guidelines for permanence and durability of the Council on Library Resources.

Printed by Data Reproductions, Inc.

Contents

Preface to the Second Edition

The inaugural volumes of *Integrated Korean*, Beginning 1 and 2, of the Korean Language Education & Research Center (KLEAR) appeared in 2000, followed in subsequent years by upper-level (Intermediate, Advanced Intermediate, Advanced, and High Advanced) volumes. The IK series, especially the beginning and intermediate volumes, have attracted a large number of learners of Korean around the world, especially in the United States and other English-speaking countries. Currently, more than seventy universities and colleges are using them for regular classroom instruction. The IK series has been popular particularly because the authors endeavored to develop all volumes in accordance with performance-based principles and methodology—contextualization, learner-centeredness, use of authentic materials, usage-orientedness, balance between acquiring and using skills, and integration of speaking, listening, reading, writing, and culture. Also, grammar points were systematically introduced with simple but adequate explanations and abundant examples and exercises.

The volumes, however, are not free from minor shortcomings that call for improvement. While using the volumes, classroom teachers and students of keen insight, as well as the authors themselves, have noticed such weaknesses here and there. The authors have felt that the volumes should be updated to better reflect the current needs of students. Consequently, at the original authors' recommendation, a revision team was formed, consisting of

Mee-Jeong Park, University of Hawai'i at Mānoa (Coordinator)
Joowon Suh, Princeton University
Mary Shin Kim, University of California at Los Angeles
Sang-suk Oh, Harvard University
Hangtae Cho, University of Minnesota

With a strong commitment to offering the best possible learning opportunities, the revision team has painstakingly reorganized and restructured the material in this second edition of the textbook based on feedback received from an extensive survey. This revised edition includes a new layout that more closely mimics the actual classroom environment, making it easier and more intuitive for both teacher and student. Both Beginning 1 and Beginning 2 now consist of more lessons, but each lesson is more focused, with fewer grammar patterns, and each of these lessons is now divided into two main sections—Conversation 1 and Conversation 2 (each with its own vocabulary list)—followed by Narration. There are more exercises that focus on vocabulary and grammar, with all exercises following our new goal of clarification and intuitiveness.

Each situation/topic-based lesson of the main texts consists of model dialogues, narration, new words and expressions, vocabulary notes, culture, grammar, usage to cover pragmatic uses, and English translation of dialogues. In response to comments from hundreds of students and instructors of the first edition, this new edition features a more attractive two-color design with all new photos and illustrations, additional lessons, and vocabulary exercises.

On behalf of KLEAR and the original authors of IK Beginning 1 and 2, I wholeheartedly thank the revision team for their indefatigable efforts and devotion.

Ho-min Sohn
KLEAR President
July 2009

Romanization

Consonants

Consonants	McCune-Reischauer	Phonetic value in IPA
ㅂ	p, b	[p,b]
ㅍ	p'	[ph]
ㅃ	pp	[p']
ㄷ	t, d	[t,d]
ㅌ	t'	[th]
ㄸ	tt	[t']
ㅅ	s	[s, ʃ]
ㅆ	ss	[s', ʃ']
ㅈ	ch, j	[c, ɟ]
ㅊ	ch'	[ch]
ㅉ	tch	[c']
ㄱ	k, g	[k,g]
ㅋ	k'	[kh]
ㄲ	kk	[k']
ㅁ	m	[m]
ㄴ	n	[n,ɲ]
ㅇ	ng	[ŋ]
ㄹ	r, l	[ɾ,l]
ㅎ	h	[h]

Vowels

Vowels/ diphthongs	McCune-Reischauer	Phonetic value in IPA
ㅣ	i	[i]
ㅟ	wi	[y,wi]
ㅔ	e	[e]
ㅖ	ye	[je]
ㅞ	we	[we]
ㅚ	oe	[Ø, we]
ㅐ	ae	[ɛ]
ㅒ	yae	[jɛ]
ㅙ	wae	[wɛ]
ㅡ	ŭ	[ɨ]
ㅓ	ŏ	[ə]
ㅕ	yŏ	[jə]
ㅝ	wŏ	[wə]
ㅏ	a	[a]
ㅑ	ya	[ja]
ㅘ	wa	[wa]
ㅜ	u	[u]
ㅠ	yu	[ju]
ㅗ	o	[o]
ㅛ	yo	[jo]
ㅢ	ŭi	[ɨ(j), i, e]

Introduction

What Kind of Language Is Korean?

This unit provides students with essential information on the linguistic features of Korean. The McCune-Reischauer system is followed in romanizing Korean expressions. Han'gŭl is provided for students who are familiar with the script.

1. Speakers
Korean is a language spoken
- a. as a native language by 67 million Korean people living on the Korean peninsula, including 23 million North Koreans and 44 million South Koreans;
- b. as a heritage language by 5.6 million overseas Korean residents, among them 2 million in China, 2 million in the United States, 0.7 million in Japan, and 0.5 million in the former Soviet Union;
- c. as a foreign language by an ever-increasing number of non-Koreans worldwide.

In terms of the number of speakers, Korean is rated eleventh among over 3,000 languages in the world.

2. Dialects
The Korean language consists of seven geographically based dialects:
- a. Central dialect (Seoul and vicinity), the standard language (*p'yojun-ŏ* 'Standard Language') of South Korea;
- b. *Ch'ungchŏng* dialect, spoken in the Ch'ungchŏng province areas located between the central and southern dialect zones;
- c. *Chŏlla* dialect, spoken in the southwest;
- d. *Kyongsang* dialect, spoken in the southeast;
- e. *P'yŏngan* dialect (P'yŏngyang and vicinity), the standard language (called *munhwa- ŏ* 'Cultured Language') of North Korea;
- f. *Hamgyŏng* dialect, spoken in the northeast;
- g. *Cheju* dialect, spoken on the island of Cheju.

Superimposed on these geographical divisions is a sociopolitical dialectal difference between North and South Korea due to the division of the country in 1945. North Koreans have replaced thousands of Chinese character–based words with newly coined native words while using many expressions laden with Communist ideology. On the other hand, South Koreans use a large number of loanwords borrowed recently from English.

Despite such geographical and sociopolitical dialectal differences, Korean is relatively homogeneous, with excellent mutual intelligibility among speakers from different areas. Mass media and formal education based on standard speech greatly contribute to the standardization of the language. Since North Korea's Pyŏngyang–based "Cultured Language" contains many elements of South Korea's Seoul-based "Standard Language," the linguistic divergence between the two Koreas is not as great as often claimed.

3. Relationship to other languages

The closest sister language of Korean is Japanese, although they are not mutually intelligible, and their relationship is much weaker than that between, say, English and French. Some scholars claim that Korean and Japanese are remotely related to the so-called Altaic languages such as native Manchu, Mongolian, and the Turkic languages. Thus, Korean and Japanese are often called Altaic languages.

Although Korea and Japan are geographically, historically, and culturally close to China, Korean and Japanese are not part of the same language family as Chinese, and therefore are not grammatically related to Chinese. However, both Korean and Japanese have borrowed a large number of Chinese words and characters throughout the course of their long historical contact with various Chinese dynasties. Such borrowed Chinese words and characters have become integral parts of the Korean and Japanese vocabularies. Since identical words and characters evolved independently in the three countries, their current pronunciations are considerably different. For example, the Chinese character words for 'Korea' and 'college' are pronounced differently in the three countries, as approximately transcribed below:

	'Korea'	'college'
Mandarin Chinese	*han-kwo*	*ta-she*
Korean	*han-guk*	*tae-hak*
Japanese	*kan-koku*	*dai-gaku*

Korea also borrowed from Japan a large number of words that the Japanese created based on Chinese characters (e.g., *yŏnghwa* 'movie', *iryoil* 'Sunday', *kwahak* 'science', *ipku* 'entrance', *yaksok* 'promise'). Numerous words have also been created by Koreans with Chinese characters as building blocks (e.g., *p'yŏnji* 'letter', *sikku* 'family members', *samch'on* 'uncle', *ilgi* 'weather', *oesang* 'on credit'). All of these Chinese character–based words are called "Sino-Korean" or "Chinese-character" words.

Since the end of World War II, Korean people have been in contact with many foreign countries and have borrowed from them thousands of words, the majority of which are English. During the thirty-five-year occupation of Korea by Japan, a considerable number of native Japanese words were also borrowed. At the same time, many Western words that the Japanese had borrowed were re-borrowed into Korean through Japanese. All such borrowed words are termed "loanwords."

4. Vocabulary

The Korean vocabulary is composed of three components: native words and affixes (approximately 35 percent), Sino-Korean words (approximately 60 percent), and loanwords (approximately 5 percent). Native words denote daily necessities (food, clothing, and shelter); locations; basic actions, activities, and states; lower-level numerals; body parts; natural objects; animals, etc. The native stock includes thousands of sound symbolic (onomatopoeic and mimetic) words and idioms and proverbs that reflect traditional culture and society. Most of the particles and affixes in Korean are from the native stock.

Due to their ideographic and monosyllabic nature, Chinese characters are easily combined and recombined to coin new terms as new cultural objects and concepts are created. Even the name of the country (*han-guk* 'Korea') is a Sino-Korean word, as we have seen above. So are most institutional terms, traditional cultural terms, personal names, and place names (except for *Seoul*, which is a native word).

There are about 14,000 loanwords in Korean, of which almost 90 percent are from English. Loanwords such as the following are commonly used in daily life, facilitating cross-cultural communication to a certain extent.

Loanword	Pronunciation	Spelling
apartment	*ap'at'ŭ*	아파트
ballpoint pen	*polp'en*	볼펜
boiler	*poillŏ*	보일러
cake	*k'eik'ŭ*	케이크
coffee	*k'ŏp'i*	커피
computer	*k'ŏmp'yut'ŏ*	컴퓨터
condo(minium)	*k'ondo*	콘도
elevator	*ellibeit'ŏ*	엘리베이터
engine	*enjin*	엔진
fax	*p'aeksŭ*	팩스
golf	*kolp'u*	골프
hotel	*hot'el*	호텔
ice cream	*aisŭk'ŭrim*	아이스크림
motorcycle	*ot'obai*	오토바이
opera	*op'era*	오페라
orange juice	*orenji jusŭ*	오렌지주스
sports	*s'ŭp'och'ŭ*	스포츠
stress	*s'ŭt'ŭresŭ*	스트레스
super(market)	*syup'ŏ*	슈퍼
taxi	*t'aeksi*	택시
television	*t'ellebijŏn*	텔레비전

Notice that the sounds of the original words are slightly modified in the loanwords according to the available sound pattern of Korean. If the words are pronounced as native speakers of the original forms normally do, they are not loanwords, but foreign words.

5. Word order

Korean, like Japanese, is a verb- or adjective-final language. The verb or adjective usually comes at the end of the sentence or clause, while all other elements, including the subject and the object, appear before the verb or adjective. In the English sentence *John plays tennis with Mary at school*, for example, *John* is the subject because it appears before the verb and denotes an entity which the rest of the sentence is about and *tennis* is its object because it appears immediately after the verb and denotes an entity that directly receives the action of the verb *plays*. The other elements (*with Mary* and *at school*) follow the object. The Korean word order would be *John school-at Mary-with tennis plays*. Notice here that while English prepositions always occur before a noun or a pronoun, Korean particles (equivalent to English prepositions) always occur *after* the element they are associated with, as in *school-at* and *Mary-with*. Korean particles are all postpositions.

Korean is often called a "free word order" language because it permits the elements before the verb or adjective to be scrambled for emphatic or other figurative purposes, as long as the verb or adjective retains the final position. Thus, for example, the neutral order of *John school-at Mary-with tennis plays* may be changed to *school-at Mary-with John tennis plays*; *Mary-with tennis John school-at plays*; *tennis John school-at Mary-with plays*; etc.

6. Situation-oriented language

Korean is often called a situation-oriented language in that contextually or situationally understood elements (including subject and object) are omitted more frequently than not. Observe the following expressions in comparison to their English counterparts and notice that the subject does not appear in any of the Korean expressions.

a. *annyŏnghaseyo?*   안녕하세요?   How are you?
   are peaceful

b. *komapsŭmnida.*   고맙습니다.   Thank you.
   am thankful

c. *ŏdi kaseyo?*   어디 가세요?   Where are you going?
   where go

Inserting the pronoun 'you' or 'I' in the above Korean expressions would sound awkward in normal contexts, unless 'you' or 'I' is emphasized or contrasted with someone else.

7. Macro-to-micro language

Korean, like Japanese, is a "macro-to-micro" language, in that the universe is represented in the order of a set (macro) and its members (micro). Thus, for example, Koreans say or write the family name first and then the given name, optionally followed by a title; say or write an address in the order of country, province, city, street, house number, and personal name; and refer to time with year first and day last.

a. *Kim Minsu kyosu-nim*   김민수 교수님   Professor Minsu Kim

b. *Sŏul Chung-gu P'il-dong 1*   서울 중구 필동 1   1 P'il Street,
Seoul Chung-district P'il-street 1   Chung District, Seoul

c. *2010-nyŏn il-wŏl i-il*   2010년 일 월 이 일   January 2, 2010
2010-year 1-month 2-day

8. Honorific expressions

Korean may be called an honorific language, in that different forms of expressions and different speech levels are used depending on the person you are talking to as well as the person you are talking about. While interpersonal differences in terms of relative age, kinship, social status, etc., are largely ignored in the structure and use of English, they are systematically encoded in the structure and use of Korean. For instance, compare English and Korean in a father and son saying good night.

English   Son: *Good night, Dad.*
           Father: *Good night, John.*

Korean   Son: *abŏji, annyŏnghi chumuseyo.*   아버지 안녕히 주무세요.
               father peacefully sleep
          Father: *nŏ do chal chara.*   너도 잘 자라.
               you also well sleep

Notice in English that son and father use the same expression except for the address terms, a kinship term by the son and a given name by the father. In Korean, on the other hand, they use entirely different expressions. Not a single element is shared. Under no circumstances may the son use any part of his father's utterance in saying good night to his father, and vice versa. Honorific and plain forms appear in the following categories.

Address/reference terms

Korean has an extensive set of address and reference terms that are sensitive to degrees of social stratification and distance between speaker and addressee and between speaker and referent. The most frequently used terms for a social superior or an adult distant equal are composed of an occupational title followed by the gender-neutral honorific suffix -*nim* 님 (lit. honorable). The full or family name may precede this.

Kim Minsu kyosu-nim	김민수 교수님	Professor Minsu Kim
Kim sŏnsaeng-nim	김 선생님	Teacher Kim
kyosu-nim	교수님	Professor

There are several title words. The most frequently used one among young company colleagues or to an adult junior is the gender-neutral noun *ssi*. This noun is attached to a full name or a given name, as follows.

Kim Yujin ssi	김유진 씨	
Yujin ssi	유진 씨	

To address or refer to a child, either a full name without any title word or a given name alone is used. Such a bare name is never used to an adult except by his/her own parent or teacher. When addressing a child by a given name, the particle *a* 아 (after a consonant) or *ya* 야 (after a vowel) is used.

Kim Yujin	김유진	(address/reference)
Minsu	민수	(address/reference)
Yujin-a!	유진아	(address)
Minsu-ya!	민수야	(address)

Honorific and humble words

A small number of commonly used words have two forms, one plain and the other honorific. The honorific forms are used for an adult equal or senior, whereas the plain forms are used for a junior or child, as illustrated below.

Plain		Honorific		
pap	밥	*chinji*	진지	'rice, meal'
chip	집	*taek*	댁	'house'
irŭm	이름	*sŏngham*	성함	'name'
nai	나이	*yŏnse*	연세	'age'
mŏk-ta	먹다	*chapsusi-da*	잡수시다	'eat'
cha-da	자다	*chumusi-da*	주무시다	'sleep'
it-ta	있다	*kyesi-da*	계시다	'stay'

There is also a small number of humble verbs used to express deference to a senior person.

Plain			Humble		
chu-da	주다	'give to a junior'	*tŭri-da*	드리다	'give to a senior'
po-da	보다	'see a junior'	*pwep-ta*	뵙다	'see a senior'

Pronouns

Korean has both plain and humble first person pronouns ('I'): *na* 나 (plain singular), *uri* 우리 (plain plural); *chŏ* 저 (humble singular), *chŏ-hŭi* 저희 (humble plural). *Chŏ* and *chŏ-hŭi are* used when talking to a senior or a socially distant adult.

There are several second person pronouns ('you') such as *nŏ* 너 (singular) and *nŏ-hŭi* (plural) addressed to children. No second person pronoun may be used to refer to an adult equal or senior. Thus, one continuing cultural observation is that Korean does not have a second person pronoun for an adult equal or senior. The only alternative is to use address/reference terms as second person pronouns, for example, *(Kim) sŏnsaeng-nim* (김) 선생님 'you teacher (Kim)'.

Speech levels

Korean has six speech levels that indicate the speaker's interpersonal relationship with the addressee. These speech levels are indicated by sentence-final suffixes attached to verbs and adjectives. These suffixes are illustrated below with the declarative (statement) sentence type. There are also interrogative (question), imperative (command, request), and propositive (suggestion) suffixes.

Speech levels	Sentence-final suffixes
deferential style	-(sŭ)mnida 습니다/ㅂ니다
polite style	-ŏyo/-ayo 어요/아요
blunt style [infrequent]	-so/-o 소/오
familiar style [infrequent]	-ne 네
intimate style	-ŏ/-a 어/아
plain style	-ta/-da 다

For example, *mŏk-sŭmnida* 먹습니다, *mŏg-ŏyo* 먹어요, *mŏk-so* 먹소, *mŏng-ne* 먹네, *mŏg-ŏ* 먹어, and *mŏng-nŭn-da* 먹는다 all mean '(someone) eats', expressed in different speech levels. Younger speakers use only the deferential, polite, intimate, and plain levels.

The most common level used to an adult is the polite one, which is less formal than but just as polite as the deferential level. While the deferential level is used mostly by male speakers, the polite level is widely used by both men and women in daily conversation. Both the polite and the deferential levels are used to address a socially equal or superior adult, but in general, the polite level is favored between close adult friends. Even in a formal situation, both the deferential and polite levels are usually used by the same speaker in the same conversation. In formal occasions such as news reports and public lectures, only the deferential level is used.

The intimate level, which is also referred to as the "half-talk" level (polite form minus -*yo* 요), may be used by an adult to a student, by a child of preschool age to his or her family members, including parents, or between close friends whose friendship began in childhood or adolescence.

The plain level is typically used by any speaker to any child, to younger siblings, children, or grandchildren regardless of age, to a daughter-in-law, between intimate adult friends whose friendship started in childhood, and in writing for a general audience. This level is frequently intermixed with the intimate level.

Subject honorific suffix

When the subject of a sentence is an adult equal or a senior, the so-called subject honorific suffix -*(ŭ)se* (으)세 before the polite ending -*yo* 요, or -*(ŭ)si* (으)시 before other suffixes, is attached to the verb or adjective, as follows:

a. *annŏngha-**se**-yo.*   (polite)   안녕하세요?   How are you?
    be peaceful

b. *annŏngha-**si**-mnikka.*   (deferential)   안녕하**십**니까?   How are you?
   be peaceful

Nonverbal behavior

Nonverbal behavior parallels the hierarchical verbal expressions. For example, one bows to a senior person such as a professor when arriving or leaving. The senior person does not bow to a junior. A junior person is required to behave properly in the presence of an ingroup senior, e.g., he or she is not to smoke in front of an ingroup senior.

9. Words and word classes

Sentences consist of words. For example, the sentence *chŏ nŭn han'gugŏ sŏnsaengnim ieyo* 저는 한국어 선생님 이에요 'I am a teacher of Korean' consists of five words: *chŏ* 저 'I', *nŭn* 는 'as for', *han'gugŏ* 한국어 'the Korean language', *sŏnsaengnim* 선생님 'a teacher', and *ieyo* 이에요 'is, are, am'. A word may consist of a single meaning unit, as in *chŏ* 'I' and *nŭn* 'as for', or may contain one or more additional elements such as suffixes, as in *han'gugŏ* 'the Korean language' (*han'guk* 'Korea' + suffix *-ŏ* 'language'), *sŏnsaengnim* 'a teacher' (*sŏnsaeng* 'a teacher' + suffix *-nim* 'Mr./Ms.'), and *ieyo* 'is, are, am' (*i* 'be' + sentence-ending suffix *-eyo* [polite level]). Based on how they function in sentences, all words are classified into the following classes and subclasses. These word classes and subclasses are given in each lesson under "New Words and Expressions."

a. **Nouns** (naming all kinds of objects, function as the grammatical subject or object of a verb or adjective):
   common nouns, e.g., *irŭm* 이름 'a name', *ch'aek* 책 'a book'
   proper nouns, e.g., *han'guk* 한국 'Korea', *Sŭt'ibŭ* 스티브 'Steve'
   counters, e.g., *kwa* 과 (counter for lessons), *mari* 마리 (counter for animals)
   loanwords, e.g., *k'ŭllaesŭ* 클래스 'a class', *pilding* 빌딩 'a building'

b. **Pronouns** (substitute for nouns or noun equivalents): e.g., *na* 나 'I' (plain), *chŏ* 저 'I' (humble), *uri* 우리 'we', *muŏt* 무엇 'what', *nugu* 누구 'who', *ibun* 이분 'this person (he/she)', *igŏs* 이것 'this (thing)'

c. **Numerals** (indicate numbers, including native and Sino-Korean words): native numbers, e.g., *hana/han* 하나/한 'one', *tul/tu* 둘/두 'two'; Sino-Korean numbers, e.g., *il* 일 'one', *i* 이 'two', *sam* 삼 'three'

d. **Verbs** (denote action or progress): e.g., *kada* 가다 'to go', *kongbuhada* 공부하다 'to study', *mŏkta* 먹다 'to eat', *poepta* 뵙다 'to see (a senior)'

e. **Adjectives** (denote state, either physical or psychological): e.g., *annyŏnghada* 안녕하다 'to be well', *mant'a* 많다 'to be much, many', *chot'a* 좋다 'to be good'

f. **Copulas** (a special subclass of adjectives, denoting equation, identification, or definition): e.g., *ita* 이다 'to be', *anita* 아니다 'to not-be'

g. **Adverbs** (modify a verb, an adjective, another adverb, a clause, a sentence, or a discourse): e.g., *aju* 아주 'very much', *yojum* 요즘 'these days', *chal* 잘 'well', *a* 아 'ah!', *ne* 네 'yes, I see', *anio* 아니요 'no'

h. **Pre-nouns** (occur only before a noun, and include demonstratives and expressions of quality and quantity): e.g., *i* 이 'this', *ku* 그 'that (near you or the subject of discussion)', *chŏ* 저 'that over there', *ŏnŭ* 어느 'which (one)', *musŭn* 무슨 'what kind of', *myŏt* 몇 'how many'

i. **Conjunctions** (connect two sentences): e.g., *kŭrigo* 그리고 'and', *kŭrŏnde* 그런데 'by the way', *kŭraeso* 그래서 'so'

j. **Particles** (following a noun or noun equivalent, indicate its grammatical relation or delimit its meaning): e.g., *i/ka* 이/가 (subject), *e* 에 'at, on, in', *ŭn/nŭn* 은/는 'as for', *to* 도 'also', *man* 만 'only'

Korean verbs and adjectives cannot stand alone; they must be followed by a sentence- or clause-ending suffix. For example, *mŏk-* 먹 'eat', *annyŏngha-* 안녕하 'be well', and *i-* 이 'be' cannot be used without an ending suffix, as in *mŏgŏyo* 먹어요 'eats', *annyŏnghaseyo* 안녕하세요 'How are you?' and *ieyo* 이에요 'is, am, are'. A bare verb or adjective form without a suffix is called a verb stem or an adjective stem. As dictionary entries, all verb and adjective stems are followed by the dictionary citation marker *-ta/-da* 다, as in *mŏkta* 먹다 'to eat', *annyŏnghada* 'to be well', and *ida* 'to be'. These are called dictionary forms.

10. The sound pattern
Korean speech sounds and the pattern of sound combinations are extremely different from English, Chinese, and Japanese. In English, for example, not only the plosive consonant sounds *p, t, ch, k,* and *s* but also their voiced counterparts *b, d, j, g,* and *z* occur in initial position in words, as in *pill/bill, tie/die, cheer/jeer, Kate/gate,* and *seal/zeal.* Korean does not allow such voiceless/voiced contrasts in initial position in words. Instead, Korean allows a three-way voiceless contrast (plain/aspirate/tense) in plosive consonants, a two-way contrast (plain/tense) in fricative consonants *s/ss* ㅅ/ㅆ, and no contrast (only plain) in the fricative consonant *h* ㅎ, as illustrated below.

a. plosive consonants:

pul	불	'fire'	*p'ul*	풀	'grass'	*ppul*	뿔	'horn'		
tal	달	'moon'	*t'al*	탈	'mask'	*ttal*	딸	'daughter'		
cha	자	'sleep'	*ch'a*	차	'kick'	*tcha*	짜	'salty'		
kae	개	'dog'	*k'ae*	캐	'dig'	*kkae*	깨	'sesame'		

b. fricative consonants:

si	시	'poem'	*ssi*	씨	'seeds'
hae	해	'sun'			

In addition to the above fifteen plosive and fricative consonants, Korean has the "liquid" consonant *l* (pronounced as flap *r*, like Japanese and Spanish *r*, in initial position or between vowels) and the nasal consonants *m* ㅁ, *n* ㄴ, and *ng* ㅇ. Thus, a total of nineteen consonants exists in Korean, as diagrammed below (with the corresponding Korean alphabetic symbols):

Manner / Place		Lips	Gum ridge	Hard palate	Soft palate	Throat
Plosive	Plain	*p* ㅂ	*t* ㄷ	*ch* ㅈ	*k* ㄱ	
	Aspirate	*p'* ㅍ	*t'* ㅌ	*ch'* ㅊ	*k'* ㅋ	
	Tense	*pp* ㅃ	*tt* ㄸ	*tch* ㅉ	*kk* ㄲ	
Fricative	Plain		*s* ㅅ			*h* ㅎ
	Tense		*ss* ㅆ			
Liquid			*l* ㄹ			
Nasal		*m* ㅁ	*n* ㄴ		*ng* ㅇ	

These nineteen consonants alter their sound values depending on their position in a word. For example, *p* ㅂ, *t* ㄷ, *ch* ㅈ, and *k* ㄱ become voiced *b, d, j,* and *g,* respectively, between voiced sounds, as in *abŏji* 아버지 'father', *pada* 바다 'sea', and *sagwa* 사과 'apple'. *hak* 학 'study' in *hak-saeng* 학생 'student' changes to *hang* in *hang-nyŏn* 학년 'school year' because the following consonant is nasal. *Kkoch'* 꽃 'flower' in *kkoch'-i* 꽃이 'flower (subject)' changes to *kkot* in *kkot-tto* 꽃도 'flower also' or when it occurs by itself, and to *kkon* in *kkon-man* 꽃만 'flower only'. These and numerous other sound-alternating phenomena will be observed and drilled in great detail throughout this volume. Notice in all of the above examples that Korean orthographic spellings are not changed despite the sound alternations.

There are eight vowel sounds in standard Korean, as represented below:

Tongue position	Front	Back	
Shape of the lips	unrounded	unrounded	rounded
High	*i* ㅣ	*ŭ* ㅡ	*u* ㅜ
Mid	*e* ㅔ	*ŏ* ㅓ	*o* ㅗ
Low	*ae* ㅐ	*a* ㅏ	

Front/back and high/mid/low refer to tongue positions, and unrounded/rounded refers to the shape of the lips in producing the relevant vowels.

There are two semivowels, *y* and *w*. Examples: *yŏngŏ* 영어 'English', *hakkyo* 학교 'school', *syup'ŏ* 슈퍼 'supermarket', *wŏryoil* 월요일 'Monday', and *kwa* 과 'lesson'.

The syllable structure of spoken Korean is outlined in (a) below, where parentheses stand for optional appearance. Only the vowel is a required element in a spoken syllable. The dot (.) stands for a spoken syllable boundary.

a.   **.(consonant) (semivowel) VOWEL (consonant).**

b.   *i*   이   'this'   *yŏl*   열 '10'   *kŭ*   그   'that'
      ot   옷   'clothes'   *pyŏl* 별 'star'

c.   *Sŏ.ul*   서울 'Seoul'   *sŏn.saeng.nim* 선생님 'teacher'
      i.rŭm   이름 'name'

While English allows up to three consonants in syllable-initial and syllable-final positions, as in "strike" and "tasks," Korean allows only one consonant in those positions. Thus, for example, the single-syllable English word *strike* is borrowed into Korean as a five-syllable loanword, *sŭ.t'ŭ.ra.i.k'ŭ* 스트라이크, with the insertion of the vowel *ŭ* 으 to make it conform to Korean syllable structure. Similarly, the final *s* ㅅ in the Korean word *kaps* 값 'price' in *kaps-i (kap.ssi)* 값이 'price (subject)' becomes silent before a consonant or when the word occurs alone, because a spoken syllable does not allow two consonants after a vowel, thus: *kap.tto* 값도 'price also' and *kap* 값 'price'.

11. Writing systems

Currently Korean is written by means of a mixed script of the Korean phonetic alphabet called Han'gŭl 한글 (meaning "the great writing") and Chinese characters. Han'gŭl is used to represent all Korean vocabulary, including native words, Sino-Korean words and loanwords, and any foreign words. Chinese characters are used only to represent Sino-Korean words. For centuries before Han'gŭl was created by King Sejong the Great, the fourth king of the Chosŏn dynasty, and his royal scholars in 1443, only Chinese characters had been used. Koreans are truly proud of Han'gŭl, one of the most scientific writing systems that has ever been created.

The current trend shows increasing use of Han'gŭl spellings over Chinese characters. Even in newspapers and scholarly books, use of Chinese characters is extremely limited. Chinese characters are often useful in differentiating the meanings of identically pronounced and spelled Han'gŭl words.

Unlike Chinese characters, which represent meanings of words, and Japanese characters, which represent syllables, the characters of the Han'gŭl alphabet represent individual sounds such as consonants and vowels. Details of Han'gŭl orthography are presented in "Han'gŭl and Pronunciation," below.

12. Learning Korean

Arabic, Chinese, Japanese, and Korean are among the most difficult languages for native English speakers to learn because of the vast differences between English and these languages in vocabulary, pronunciation, grammar, and writing system, as well as in the underlying tradition, culture, and society. English speakers require three times as much time to learn these "difficult" languages as to learn "easy" languages, such as French or Spanish, to attain a comparable level of proficiency. Indeed, English-speaking students who study Korean deserve praise for undertaking such a difficult but invaluable language, which has enormous cultural, academic, economic, and strategic significance.

한글 Han'gŭl

In this unit, students learn how the individual letters and syllable blocks of the Korean alphabet, Han'gŭl (한글), are written and pronounced, how the Korean alphabetic letters are ordered in dictionaries, word lists, and indexes, and how correct pronunciations are obtained from a variety of Han'gŭl spellings by means of a simple set of pronunciation rules. Students will also learn how to romanize Han'gŭl according to the McCune-Reischauer system of romanization, which is widely used by scholars, library cataloguers, and the educated public in English-speaking countries.

1. Introduction

Korean speech sounds are graphically represented by Han'gŭl letters. The individual consonant and vowel letters of Han'gŭl are combined into syllable blocks to spell Korean words and sentences. For example, the consonant sound *h* is represented by the Han'gŭl letter ㅎ, the vowel sound *a* by the letter ㅏ, and the consonant sound *n* by the letter ㄴ. The three letters ㅎ, ㅏ, and ㄴ are combined as the syllable block 한 to be pronounced *han*, which means 'one' or 'great' in Korean.

Similarly, the consonant *k* or *g* is represented by ㄱ, the vowel *ŭ* by ㅡ (pronounced somewhat like English *u* in *put* and *oo* in *good*), and the consonant *l* (like English *l* in *please*) by ㄹ. These letters are combined as 글 and pronounced *kŭl* or *gŭl*. This syllable means 'writing' or 'script'. The two syllable blocks 한글 are pronounced as *han.gul*, which means 'the great writing', the literal name of the Korean alphabet.

ㅎ + ㅏ + ㄴ	=	한	*han*
ㄱ + ㅡ + ㄹ	=	글	*kŭl/gŭl*
한 + 글	=	한글	*han.gŭl*

Remember that a syllable must contain one and only one vowel. Since the word 한글 has two vowels, it has two syllables.

Notice in the above that ㄱ is pronounced as either *k* or *g*. When ㄱ is preceded and followed by "voiced" (vocal-cord vibrating) sounds such as a vowel or *n, m, ng,* or *l*, it is pronounced as the voiced sound *g,* as in 한글 *han.gŭl* where ㄴ *n* and ㅡ *ŭ* are voiced sounds. Otherwise it is pronounced as a voiceless *k,* as in the independently pronounced 글 *kŭl* or 학 *hak.* Similarly, the letter ㄹ is associated with two sounds, *l* and *r* (flap *r* like American English *t* in *water* and Japanese and Spanish *r*). It is pronounced as *l* when it appears at the end of a syllable, as in 글 *kŭl.* It is pronounced as *r* between two vowels, as in 나라 *na.ra* 'country'. We will see more on the pronunciations of ㄹ later.

Practice 1
Transcribe the following syllable blocks in Roman letters in the spaces provided.

할	날	각	간
근	흔	는	흑
가난	그늘	나는	극한
하늘	나를	가락	흔한

Practice 2
Write the following in 한글.

han.gŭl	*kŭ.rŭl*	*nan.gan*
kŭn.hak	*ha.na*	*kŭ.nŭl*

한글 is written either horizontally across the page, as in this book, or vertically, as in many South Korean newspapers. In North Korea, only the horizontal writing is practiced.

2. Vowel letters

Letter shapes
한글 consists of vowel and consonant letters corresponding to vowel and consonant sounds in Korean speech. All vowel letters are composed of one or more of three kinds of strokes: a long vertical stroke (ㅣ), a long horizontal stroke (ㅡ), and a short horizontal or vertical stroke (￢ or ㅣ). The short stroke was originally a round dot (·). The three basic strokes were modeled after the cosmological philosophy of heaven (·), earth (ㅡ), and human being (ㅣ).

한글 has six simple letters and two compound letters to represent eight simple vowel sounds. (We have seen that the spelling 한글 contains two of these vowel letters, ㅏ and ㅡ.)

Simple letters	ㅏ	ㅓ	ㅗ	ㅜ	ㅡ	ㅣ
	a	*ŏ*	*o*	*u*	*ŭ*	*i*
Compound letters	ㅐ	ㅔ				
	ae	*e*				

ㅐ is the combination of ㅏ and ㅣ, and ㅔ is the combination of ㅓ and ㅣ. In fact, when 한글 was created, ㅐ was pronounced as *ay* and ㅔ as *ŏy*. They have subsequently evolved into the simple vowels *ae* and *e*, respectively.

The short stroke is placed horizontally on a long vertical vowel stroke, as in ㅏ and ㅓ and vertically on a long horizontal stroke, as in ㅗ and ㅜ. The vowel sounds with a short stroke on the right or above a long stroke (ㅏ and ㅗ) are called "bright" vowels, whereas the vowels with a short stroke on the left or below a long stroke (ㅓ and ㅜ) are called "dark" vowels, because the former sounds are perceived as brighter or more sonorous to native speakers than the latter. The vowels represented by ㅡ and ㅣ are neutral vowels. A bright vowel and a dark vowel are not combined in a single syllable block in making a diphthong.

Bright vowels	ㅏ ㅗ
Dark vowels	ㅓ ㅜ
Neutral vowels	ㅡ ㅣ

Of the eight vowel letters given above, five are upright or vertical whereas the remaining three are lying or horizontal. In writing a syllable block, an initial consonant letter is placed on the left side of a vertical vowel letter, as in 한, and on top of a horizontal vowel letter, as in 글.

Practice 3
The basic stroke order in 한글 orthography is left to right and top to bottom, as in Chinese characters. Practice the orders:

ㅏ	ㅣ	⇒	ㅏ			ㅓ	ㅡ	⇒	ㅓ		
ㅗ	ㅣ	⇒	ㅗ			ㅜ	ㅡ	⇒	ㅜ		
ㅐ	ㅣ	⇒	ㅏ	⇒	ㅐ	ㅔ	ㅡ	⇒	ㅓ	⇒	ㅔ
한	ㅎ	⇒	하	⇒	한	글	ㄱ	⇒	그	⇒	글

Vowel pronunciation
The qualities of Korean vowels are not the same as those of English vowels, although they can be approximated as follows.

ㅏ	a	*father, yarn* (shorter than this *a*)
ㅓ	ŏ	*awake, young* (with the root of the tongue pulled back)
ㅗ	o	*own* (without the *w*-color)
ㅜ	u	*boo, you* (shorter than this *oo* or *ou*)
ㅡ	ŭ	*houses, put* (like ㅜ but without lip-rounding)
ㅣ	i	*see* (shorter than this *ee*)
ㅐ	ae	*care*
ㅔ	e	*met, yes*

The eight simple vowels of Korean may be arranged in box form as follows.

ㅣ	ㅡ	ㅜ
ㅔ	ㅓ	ㅗ
ㅐ	ㅏ	

Each vowel is located at the approximate place where it is articulated in the mouth. For example, the vowel ㅣ *i* is produced when the top of the tongue approaches the hard palate, the vowel ㅜ *u* when the back of the tongue approaches the rear part of the soft palate, and the vowel ㅏ *a* when the space between the back of the lowered tongue and the soft palate is widened. Only ㅜ and ㅗ are pronounced with the lips rounded.

Practice 4
Listen to and repeat after the instructor in producing the eight vowels. Notice the tongue positions for each vowel. Pay attention to the different spacings between the tongue and the palate.

The vowels ㅔ *e* and ㅐ *ae* are very similar. Although they can be distinguished by careful pronunciation when you repeat after your instructor, both of these vowels are pronounced indistinguishably by many speakers in casual speech as a sound between *e* and *ae*. However, the difference is maintained in writing, as in 게 'crab' and 개 'dog'.

Since accurate pronunciation of the eight vowels is essential in learning spoken Korean, make a special effort to keep English pronunciation from interfering with your learning of Korean vowels. Completely master the pronunciations of the eight basic vowels through intensive practice with your instructor and via tape recording.

Practice 5
Listen to your instructor and identify the vowels he or she is pronouncing.

(a) 가   (b) 개   (c) 거   (d) 게
(e) 고   (f) 구   (g) 그   (h) 기

Practice 6
Listen to and pronounce each of the following pairs many times. Have your pronunciations checked by the instructor.

(a) 가, 거   (b) 거, 고   (c) 그, 거   (d) 고, 그
(e) 그, 구   (f) 구, 고   (g) 게, 거   (h) 개, 가

Practice 7
Listen to your instructor, and write down the syllable blocks in the order you hear them.

Examples: (a) 고, 그, 거, 구   (b) 누, 노, 너, 느
            (c) 허, 흐, 호, 후   (d) 글, 걸, 갈, 굴, 골

There is a distinction between short and long vowels in many words, although this distinction is not represented in 한글 orthography. For example, when 눈 is pronounced short, it means 'eye', whereas when it is pronounced long, it means 'snow'. Similarly, a short 밤 is 'night' and a long 밤 is 'chestnut'; and a short 말 is 'horse' and a long 말 is 'language'. This short-long distinction, which is relatively strict in the speech of the older generation, has disappeared in the speech of the younger generation.

3. Diphthong (semivowel + vowel) letters

Diphthongs with the semivowel y
One additional short stroke makes each of the six single-letter vowels a diphthong with *y*, as follows. Remember that stroke order is top to bottom and left to right.

Simple vowel ⇒ diphthong			Stroke order					
ㅏ	⇒	ㅑ	*ya*	ㅣ	⇒	ㅏ	⇒	ㅑ
ㅓ	⇒	ㅕ	*yŏ*	─	⇒	=	⇒	ㅕ
ㅗ	⇒	ㅛ	*yo*	ㅣ	⇒	ㅣㅣ	⇒	ㅛ
ㅜ	⇒	ㅠ	*yu*	─	⇒	ㅜ	⇒	ㅠ
ㅐ	⇒	ㅒ	*yae*	ㅣ	⇒	ㅏ	⇒	ㅑ	⇒	ㅒ
ㅔ	⇒	ㅖ	*ye*	─	⇒	=	⇒	ㅕ	⇒	ㅖ

The distinction between ㅐ and ㅔ is lost in casual speech, both being pronounced as ㅔ, but is retained in writing as well as in extremely careful pronunciation.

Practice 8
Repeat after your instructor in pronouncing the following syllable blocks several times, and then identify in writing the ones pronounced by your instructor.

야,   겨,   교,   규,   개,   계

Practice 9
Read the following syllables in the order given until you become completely fluent. Dictionary entries follow this order.

가,   개,   갸,   걔,   거,   게,   겨,   계,

고,   교,   구,   규,   그,   기

Diphthongs with the semivowel w and the diphthong ŭi
There are six diphthongs beginning with the sound *w* (as in English *week*, *Washington*, *work*). These are graphically expressed by combining two simple vowel letters. The letters ㅗ and ㅜ are used to represent the semivowel sound *w*. There is an idiosyncratic diphthong which consists of ㅡ and ㅣ.

Simple vowel	+	Simple vowel	=	Diphthong	
ㅗ	+	ㅏ	=	와	*wa*
ㅗ	+	ㅐ	=	왜	*wae*
ㅗ	+	ㅣ	=	외	*we*
ㅜ	+	ㅓ	=	워	*wŏ*
ㅜ	+	ㅔ	=	웨	*we*
ㅜ	+	ㅣ	=	위	*wi*
ㅡ	+	ㅣ	=	의	*ŭi*

Practice 10
Practice proper stroke order in writing the combinations above.

Example: ㅣ   ⇒   ㅗ   ⇒   외   ⇒   와

The letters 외 and 웨, which used to be pronounced differently, are now pronounced identically as *we*, although the distinction is kept in writing.
    Combinations of ㅗ + ㅓ, ㅗ + ㅔ, ㅜ + ㅏ, and ㅜ + ㅐ are not permitted. This is due to the so-called vowel harmony principle in Korean, which does not allow a bright vowel (ㅏ, ㅗ) to be combined with a dark vowel (ㅜ, ㅓ) within a syllable, although either may combine with the neutral vowel ㅣ, as in ㅐ, ㅔ, 외, and 위. Thus, for example, the syllable blocks 과, 궈, 괘, and 궤 are acceptable, whereas 고ㅓ, 구ㅏ, 고ㅔ, and 구ㅐ are not.
    The diphthong 의 is unstable and is pronounced as *ŭ* or *ŭi* (in word-initial position not preceded by a consonant) and *i* (in non-initial position and after a consonant in initial position). For example, the word 의논 'discussion' is pronounced as *ŭ.non* or *ŭi.non* (ㅇ in the syllable block 의 is a silent or zero consonant). 흰 'white' is pronounced only as *hin* because 의 is preceded by a consonant, ㅎ. (In addition, the possessive particle 의 'of' is uniquely pronounced like 에 *e*.)

Practice 11

Repeat after your instructor in pronouncing the following syllable blocks several times, and then write down the ones pronounced by the instructor.

화,   왜,   외,   희,   워,   웨,   위

Practice 12

Read and write the following syllable blocks many times in the order given. This is the order that Korean students learn for dictionary and other uses.

(a)   가,   개,   갸,   걔,

(b)   거,   게,   겨,   계,

(c)   고,   과,   괘,   괴,   교

(d)   구,   궈,   궤,   귀,   규

(e)   그,   긔,   기

4. Consonant letters

Letter shapes

There are nineteen consonant letters. Consonant letters originally depicted the speech organs that produce consonant sounds: the lips, tooth, tongue, and throat. The shapes of these organs are associated with the following five consonant letters.

    ㅁ *m*:   lips

    ㄴ *n*:   tongue tip touching the gum ridge

    ㅅ *s*:   tooth (for hissing sounds)

    ㄱ *k/g*: tongue back touching the soft palate

    ㅇ *ng*: throat

    The remaining fourteen consonants are produced in the same general areas as the above five places of articulation. Thus, the letters representing the sounds related to the above five sounds are derived by adding extra strokes to the basic letters.

Lip sounds

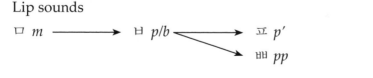

Gum ridge (alveolar) sounds

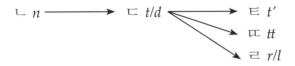

Hissing sounds (hard-palate sounds)

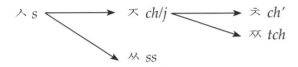

Soft-palate (velar) and throat sounds

ㅇ *ng* ⟶ ㅎ *h*

Practice 13
Write the nineteen consonant letters repeatedly until you are able to remember them along with the romanized letters. In writing the letters, follow the correct stroke order, keeping the principle of left to right and top to bottom in mind.

Consonant pronunciation
Of the nineteen consonant letters given above, the sound qualities of the four letters ㅁ, ㄴ, ㅇ, and ㅎ are essentially the same as in English: *m* (as in *map, team*), *n* (as in *nose, moon*), *ng* (as in *song, king*), and *h* (as in *hit, hope*), respectively. The only exception is that ㄴ is pulled to the hard-palate position before the palatal vowel *i* or the semivowel *y*, as in 언니 and 안녕. This pronunciation is called palatalization, in that ㄴ is assimilated to the palatal vowel or semivowel.

The sound quality of ㄹ is very different from that of either English *l* or English *r*, although ㄹ is romanized as *r/l*. In word-initial position, between two vowels, or between a vowel and the consonant ㅎ, ㄹ is pronounced as a so-called flap *r* like the Japanese or Spanish *r*. Examples: 라디오 *radio*, 나라 *nara*, and 말한다 *maranda*. In word-final position, between a vowel and a consonant, or when adjacent to another ㄹ, it is pronounced like the so-called English light *l* that appears before a vowel (e.g., *lung, slope*). Example: 말 *mal*, 말과 *mal.gwa*, and

빨리 *ppal.li*. In 나를 *na.rŭl*, for example, the first ㄹ in 를 is pronounced as a flap *r* and the second ㄹ as a light *l*. In no situation does a so-called dark *l* (e.g., *milk, bill*) appear in Korean. This is the reason Koreans have difficulty pronouncing English words with a dark *l* occurring in syllable-final position, and English speakers have difficulty producing Korean light *l* when it occurs after a vowel. When two ㅁ's, ㄴ's, or ㄹ's occur in sequence, each ㅁ, ㄴ, or ㄹ is pronounced distinctly, as in 감미 *kam.mi*, 반날 *pan.nal*, and 불량 *pul.lyang*.

Practice 14
Repeat the following words after the instructor several times. Then pronounce them as directed.

(a)	마음	(b)	엄마	(c)	한강	(d)	만남
(e)	김치	(f)	노래	(g)	라일락	(h)	마을
(i)	사람	(j)	안녕	(k)	영어	(l)	밀크

Korean has two distinctive kinds of s-sounds: plain ㅅ and tensed ㅆ, which is tense in the sense that the speech organs involved become tensed for its articulation. The tense ㅆ has the sound quality similar to the initial *s* in English words like *sun* and *sea*, where *s* is followed by a vowel, whereas the plain ㅅ is similar in sound quality to the *s* in words like *strong, spoil,* and *steam,* where *s* is followed by a consonant. While English *s* is pronounced with the tip of the tongue approaching the gum-ridge area, the Korean ㅅ and ㅆ are produced with the top of the tongue approaching the gum ridge and front part of the hard palate and the tongue tip touching the lower teeth. Both ㅅ and ㅆ are pronounced in the back part of the hard palate when they are followed by the palatal vowel *i* or semivowel *y*, as in 시, 쉬, 씨 and 샤쓰.

Practice 15
Pronounce the following pairs with particular attention to the plain and tense distinction, on one hand, and the palatalized and unpalatalized distinction, on the other.
Then write the words in 한글 as they are pronounced by the instructor.

(a)	사다	싸다
(b)	살	쌀
(c)	시름	씨름
(d)	시계	셔츠

The following twelve plosive consonants are contrasted with one another depending on whether they are pronounced with a puff of air (aspirated) and whether they are pronounced with muscle tension (tense) in the relevant speech organs. If neither quality is present, they are plain consonants.

Plain	Aspirated	Tense
ㅂ	ㅍ	ㅃ
ㄷ	ㅌ	ㄸ
ㅈ	ㅊ	ㅉ
ㄱ	ㅋ	ㄲ

In word-initial position in English, only the aspirated consonants corresponding exactly to the four aspirated Korean consonants occur, as in *pill, tall, church,* and *king.* In Korean, however, all plain, aspirated, and tense consonants occur in word-initial position. Thus, English speakers have no problem in pronouncing the four Korean aspirated consonants (ㅍ, ㅌ, ㅊ, ㅋ), but they need much practice to master the plain and tense sounds.

The Korean tense consonants ㅃ, ㄸ, ㅉ, and ㄲ are very similar to the underlined consonants in English words such as *speak, steam, midget,* and *skill,* respectively.

As for the plain set of plosive consonants, if you can eliminate the puff of air (aspiration) from the initial consonants in *pill, tall, church,* and *king,* you can pronounce Korean ㅂ, ㄷ, ㅈ, and ㄱ, respectively. Your instructor will tell you whether you are producing the Korean plain consonants correctly.

The plain consonants ㅂ, ㄷ, ㅈ, and ㄱ (but not ㅅ) undergo sound change in certain environments. When they are preceded and followed by voiced sounds such as vowels and nasal consonants, they are assimilated to these sounds and pronounced as the voiced sounds *b, d, j,* and *g,* respectively, as in 한번 더 *han. bŏn.dŏ,* 놀자 *nol.ja,* and 한국 *han.guk.* In other environments they are voiceless, as in 밥 *pap,* 다시 *ta.si,* 질문 *chil.mun,* and 가요 *ka.yo.* In 부부 *pubu,* for example, the first 부 is articulated with a voiceless ㅂ *p* and the second 부 with a voiced ㅂ *b.*

Practice 16
Pronounce the following words with voiced and voiceless plain consonants.

ㅂ :   밥   바람   바보   공부   일본   가방

ㄷ :   달   대학   도둑   바다   어디   라디오

ㅈ :   집   질문   중국   자주   사전   어제

ㄱ :   길   교실   공책   가게   미국   불고기

Practice 17

Repeat after your instructor several times and have your pronunciations checked. Then identify, first verbally and then through spelling, the words the instructor pronounces from the following list.

(a) 불   풀   뿔
(b) 달   탈   딸
(c) 자다   차다   짜다
(d) 근   큰   끈

5. Syllable-block building

한글 letters are combined into syllable blocks. As has been observed, a square syllable block has one initial consonant position (C) followed by one vowel or diphthong position. In the final consonant (받침 *pat'ch'im*) position, one or two consonants may occur.

If a syllable does not have an initial consonant, the syllable block must have the letter ○ in the initial consonant position, as in 안 *an* or 위 *wi*. ○ is silent and functions as a zero consonant in the initial position of a syllable block. If the vowel letter in the syllable block contains only one or two long vertical strokes, it is written to the right of the initial consonant letter.

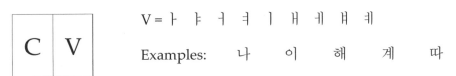

V = ㅏ ㅑ ㅓ ㅕ ㅣ ㅐ ㅔ ㅒ ㅖ

Examples: 나   이   해   계   따

If the vowel letter in the syllable block contains only a long horizontal stroke, the vowel letter is written below the initial consonant letter.

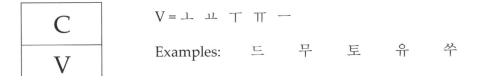

V = ㅗ ㅛ ㅜ ㅠ ㅡ

Examples: 드   무   토   유   쑤

If a diphthong letter contains a long horizontal stroke and a long vertical stroke, the initial consonant letter occurs in the upper left corner.

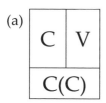   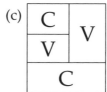

$V_{1+}V_2 =$ 놔 ᅯ ᅬ ᅫ ᅰ ᅱ ᅴ

Examples: 뵈   왜   희   풰   쉬

When a syllable has one or two final consonants (받침), they follow one of the following three models:

(a) | C | V |
    | C(C) | |

(b) | C |
    | V |
    | C(C) |

(c) | C | V |
    | V | |
    | C | |

Examples:

(a)   김   깎   값   젊   많

(b)   돈   꼭   볶   흙   굶

(c)   흰   뵙   꿩   봤

As final consonants (받침), the following two-letter combinations are available in addition to single-consonant letters:

ㄲ, ㅆ, ㄳ, ㄵ, ㄶ, ㄺ, ㄻ, ㄼ, ㄽ, ㄾ, ㄿ, ㅀ, ㅄ

In writing, the shape and size of the letters in syllable blocks should be balanced to fill the space.

Practice 18
Compose 한글 syllable blocks that correspond to the following romanized spellings.

pu.bu		kim.ch'i		o.ren.ji	
mi.guk		ma.ra.t'on		kal.bi	
Talk		k'ŏ.p'i.syop		ppal.lae	
kulm.ŏ		ŭlp'.ta		kang.a.ji	

Practice 19
Pronounce the following and observe the differences between Korean and English pronunciations of the given words. Discuss in class the possible reasons for the pronunciation differences.

(a)	아메리카	(b)	캐나다	(c)	잉글랜드
(d)	이탈리아	(e)	프랑스	(f)	브라질
(g)	뉴질랜드	(h)	말레이시아	(i)	코리아
(j)	오렌지	(k)	스트레스	(l)	비타민
(m)	마스크	(n)	오스트레일리아		

6. Summary of 한글 letters

Vowels			Consonants	
Simple	ㅏ ㅓ ㅗ ㅜ ㅡ ㅣ		Simple	ㄱ ㄴ ㄷ ㄹ ㅁ
	ㅐ ㅔ			ㅂ ㅅ ㅇ ㅈ
Diphthongs	y + vowel	ㅑ ㅕ ㅛ ㅠ ㅒ ㅖ	Aspirated	ㅊ ㅋ ㅌ ㅍ ㅎ
	w + vowel	ㅘ ㅙ ㅚ ㅝ ㅞ ㅟ	Tense	ㄲ ㄸ ㅃ ㅆ ㅉ
	ŭ + i	ㅢ		

7. Alphabetic order and the names of the letters

한글 letters are alphabetically ordered for dictionary entries, directories, word lists, and indexes (as in this book). Each letter has a name. In the following tables, boldface letters are relatively more basic than the other letters.

Vowel and diphthong letters												
Order	ㅏ	ㅐ	ㅑ	ㅒ	ㅓ	ㅔ	ㅕ	ㅖ	ㅗ	ㅘ	ㅙ	ㅚ
Name	아	애	야	얘	어	에	여	예	오	와	왜	외
Name	a	ae	ya	yae	ŏ	e	yŏ	ye	o	wa	wae	we

Order	ㅛ	ㅜ	ㅝ	ㅞ	ㅟ	ㅠ	ㅡ	ㅢ	ㅣ
Name	요	우	워	웨	위	유	으	의	이
Name	yo	u	wŏ	we	wi	yu	ŭ	ŭi	i

Consonant letters										
Order	ㄱ	ㄲ	ㄴ	ㄷ	ㄸ	ㄹ	ㅁ	ㅂ	ㅃ	ㅅ
Name	기역	쌍기역	니은	디귿	쌍디귿	리을	미음	비읍	쌍비읍	시옷
Name	ki.yŏk	ssang ki.yŏk	ni.ŭn	ti.gŭt	ssang ti.gŭt	ri.ŭl	mi.ŭm	pi.ŭp	ssang pi.ŭp	si.ot

Order	ㅆ	ㅇ	ㅈ	ㅉ	ㅊ	ㅋ	ㅌ	ㅍ	ㅎ
Name	쌍시옷	이응	지읒	쌍지읒	치읓	키읔	티읕	피읖	히읗
Name	ssang si.ot	i.ŭng	chi.ŭt	ssang chi.ŭt	ch'i.ŭt	k'i.ŭk	t'i.ŭt	p'i.ŭp	hi.ŭt

Notice that the name of each consonant letter begins and ends with the sound in question. Notice further that, for certain consonants, their sound quality when ending a name is not the same as when beginning a name: ㅅ (시옷 si.ot), ㅈ (지읒 chi.ŭt), ㅊ (치읓 ch'i.ŭt), ㅋ (키읔 k'i. ŭk), ㅌ (티읕 t'i.ŭt), ㅍ (피읖 p'i.ŭp), and ㅎ (히읗 hi.ŭt). This is due to the "unrelease" or "closure" of word-final consonants in Korean. For example, when 옷 is pronounced without releasing the speech organs involved for ㅅ, the outcome is ot.

As the name 이응 i.ŭng indicates, ㅇ has two functions. It has a silent or zero quality in syllable-initial position, as in 이 i. It simply fills the zero consonant position in a syllable block that begins with a vowel sound. When it occurs in syllable-final position, it has the nasal quality ng.

The term 쌍 ssang means 'twin'. This is to indicate that the same letter is doubled to represent tenseness.

Han'gŭl: Pronunciation Rules

The 한글 spelling convention follows the principle of spelling a lexical item (that is, word element) in one fixed way, regardless of its pronunciation changes in different combinations with other lexical items. For example, 'Korea' is pronounced *han.guk* and spelled 한국. When this word is followed by 말 'language' to mean 'the Korean language', the pronunciation of *han.guk* changes to *han.gung* 'Korea' as in *han.gung.mal* 'the Korean language' because of the assimilation of *k* to the following nasal consonant, *m*. Yet the spelling is 한국말, not 한궁말. This is similar to the English practice of expressing past action with *-ed* despite the fact that pronunciations vary depending on the phonetic environments, as in *kicked, nibbled*, and *knitted*. Since the sound changes are predictable given relevant sound environments, the student needs a set of simple rules for pronouncing words written in 한글. The following rules are basic and essential for the beginning student.

Rule 1. Resyllabification

When a syllable-final consonant is followed without pause by a vowel in the following syllable, that consonant is carried over to the following syllable to function as its initial consonant in pronunciation. The following syllable may be a part of a suffix or another word. This linking of syllable-final consonant to following syllable in pronunciation is technically called "resyllabification." For example, 한글로 does not show any linking, but 한글은 is pronounced [한그른]. In this case, the sound quality of ㄹ changes from *l* to *r* because ㄹ now appears between two vowels. Similarly, when a syllable block ends in a double consonant letter, the second consonant is carried over to the following vowel-initial syllable in pronunciation, as in 읽어요 [일거요].

Practice 1

(a)	책을 펴세요 [채글 펴세요]	(b)	알았어요 [아라써요]
(c)	질문이 있어요	(d)	읽어 보세요
(e)	잘 들으세요	(f)	맞았어요
(g)	앉으세요	(h)	천만에요
(i)	책이 이 층에 없어요	(j)	영어를 쓰지 마세요
(k)	백화점에 갔어요	(l)	옷을 받았어요

Rule 2. Syllable-final closure (unrelease)

At the end of a word or before a consonant, all Korean consonants are pronounced with closure of the speech organs involved, that is, without releasing air. As a result, sound changes occur in consonants in word-final or pre-consonantal position. For example, 꽃은 'as for flowers' is pronounced as *kko.ch'ŭn* without any change in ㅊ because the word 꽃 'flower' is immediately followed by the vowel-initial particle 은 'as for'. However, 꽃 'flower' and 꽃도 'flower also' are pronounced [꼳] *kkot* and [꼳또] *kkot.tto*, respectively, and not as *kkoch* and *kkoch.to*. The change of ㅊ *ch* to ㄷ *t* here happens because the speech organs (the tongue and the hard palate) responsible for the articulation of the word-final and pre-consonantal ㅊ are not released. Thus, the following changes occur in the same positions.

Lips	ㅂ, ㅍ	→	[ㅂ]
Gum ridge and hard palate	ㄷ, ㅌ, ㅅ, ㅆ, ㅈ, ㅊ →		[ㄷ]
Soft palate	ㄱ, ㅋ, ㄲ	→	[ㄱ]

Practice 2

(a)	잎이 [이피]	잎 [입]		잎과 [입꽈]
(b)	같아요	같지요		
(c)	옷을	옷		옷도
(d)	갔어	갔다		갔지
(e)	낮에	밤낮		낮과
(f)	빛이	빛		빛조차
(g)	부엌에	부엌		부엌 바닥
(h)	낚아요	낚시		낚다가
(i)	꽃이	꽃		꽃씨

The only consonant sounds that occur at the end of a word or before another consonant are the seven simple consonants ㅂ, ㄷ, ㄱ, ㅁ, ㄴ, ㅇ, and ㄹ.

Rule 3. Nasal assimilation

All plosive and fricative consonants become the corresponding nasal consonants before a nasal consonant (ㅁ, ㄴ), as indicated below. Notice that even ㅎ is included in the change.

ㅂ, ㅍ	→	[ㅁ]
ㄷ, ㅌ, ㅅ, ㅆ, ㅈ, ㅊ, ㅎ	→	[ㄴ]
ㄱ, ㅋ, ㄲ	→	[ㅇ]

Practice 3

(a)	입만 [임만]	(b)	앞문
(c)	없나요	(d)	받는다
(e)	끝나다	(f)	몇 년
(g)	있는데	(h)	일학년
(i)	낳는다	(j)	모르겠습니다
(k)	한국말로 뭐라고 합니까	(l)	여기서 끝내겠습니다

Rule 4. ㄴ to ㄹ assimilation

When ㄹ and ㄴ come together, the ㄴ sound is usually replaced by the ㄹ sound, as in 칠 년 [칠런]. When ㄹ is followed by the vowel *i* or the semivowel *y* in some compound words, another ㄹ is inserted between them, as in 물약 [물략].

Practice 4

(a)	진리	(b)	신라
(c)	전라도	(d)	달님
(e)	팔 년	(f)	서울역
(g)	길 이름		

Rule 5. Tensification

When a plain plosive consonant (ㅂ, ㄷ, ㅈ, ㄱ) or the fricative consonant ㅅ is preceded by a plosive or fricative consonant, it is reinforced to become a corresponding tense consonant, as in 몇 번 [면뻔] (careful speech) or [며뻔] (casual speech), 학생 [학쌩] and 없다 [업따].

Practice 5

(a)	몇 과	(b)	식당
(c)	학교	(d)	숙제
(e)	꽃집	(f)	책상

(g)   몇 시간   (h)   처음 뵙겠습니다
(i)   질문이 없습니다

Tensification also occurs in compound nouns. This and other kinds of reinforcement will be discussed later.

Practice 6

(a)	여름 방학	[여름빵악]
(b)	길가	[길까]
(c)	강가	[강까]
(d)	봄비	[봄삐]
(e)	누구 거예요?	[누구 꺼예요]
(f)	마이클 거예요	[마이클 꺼예요]

Rule 6. Aspiration and /ㅎ/ weakening

The fricative consonant ㅎ is produced in the throat, soft palate, hard palate, or lips depending on the following vowel. When it is followed or preceded by a plain plosive consonant (ㅂ, ㄷ, ㅈ, ㄱ), it merges with the consonant to produce the corresponding aspirate consonant (ㅍ, ㅌ, ㅊ, ㅋ), as in 좋다 [조타] and 닫히다 [다치다].

ㅎ + ㅂ, ㄷ, ㅈ, ㄱ	= [ㅍ, ㅌ, ㅊ, ㅋ]
ㅂ, ㄷ, ㅈ, ㄱ + ㅎ	= [ㅍ, ㅌ, ㅊ, ㅋ]

Practice 7

(a)	좋고	(b)	입학
(c)	많다	(d)	좋지 않다
(e)	책하고	(f)	시작합시다
(g)	어떻게	(h)	꽃하고
(i)	대답하세요		

Between two voiced sounds (vowels, nasals, or ㄹ consonants), ㅎ tends to become silent in casual speech, as in 좋아요 [조아요] and 말한다 [마란다].

Practice 8

(a)	전화	(b)	여름 방학
(c)	사랑한다	(d)	안녕하세요
(e)	많아요	(f)	좋았어요
(g)	잘했어요	(h)	천천히 말해 보세요
(i)	감사합니다	(j)	괜찮아요

Rule 7. Double consonant reduction

As indicated under rule 1, the second of the two consonants at the syllable-final position (e.g., 값, 없, 읽, 않, 덟, 앉) is carried over to the following syllable in pronunciation if this syllable does not have an initial consonant, as in 값이 [갑씨]. However, one of the two consonants becomes silent at the end of a word or before a consonant, as in 값 [갑] and 값도 [갑또]. Unlike in English where up to three consonants may occur in sequence in a syllable (e.g., *street*, *masks*), even a cluster of two consonants is not allowed in a single Korean syllable.

It is difficult to predict which of two syllable-final consonants will become silent. Normally the silent consonant is the second one, but there are exceptions.

Practice 9

(a)	여덟	[여덜]
(b)	없다	[업따]
(c)	책을 읽습니다	[채글 익씁니다] or [채글 일씁니다]
(d)	질문이 없습니다	[질무니 업씁니다]
(e)	괜찮습니다	[괜찬씀니다]
(f)	앉겠어요	[안께써요]

Rule 8. Palatalization

When a word ending in ㄷ or ㅌ is followed by a suffix beginning with the vowel *i* or the semivowel *y* (whether ㅎ intervenes or not), the ㄷ and ㅌ are pronounced ㅈ and ㅊ, respectively, as in 닫혀요 [다처요] and 붙이다 [부치다]. This change is technically called "palatalization" because the original gum-ridge consonants are articulated in the area of the hard palate.

Practice 10

(a)	붙어요	붙여요
(b)	다 같아요	다 같이 가요
(c)	밑에	밑이

Rule 9. Place assimilation

In casual speech, [ㄷ] is optionally pronounced [ㅂ] before ㅂ or ㅃ and as [ㄱ] before ㄱ or ㄲ, as in 꽃병 [꼳뼝/꼽뼝] and 갔고 [간꼬/각꼬]. Similarly, [ㄴ] is optionally pronounced [ㅁ] before ㅂ, ㅃ, or ㅁ, and [ㅇ] before ㄱ or ㄲ, as in 한미 [한미/함미], 빗물 [빈물/빔물], and 한강 [한강/항강].

Practice 11

(a)	옷감	(b)	신문
(c)	옷빨래	(d)	한국어
(e)	젖병	(f)	눈꺼풀
(g)	닫고	(h)	꽃무늬
(i)	밭갈이	(j)	신발

Useful Classroom Expressions

Here are some basic expressions that you will hear and use frequently in the classroom context. They are not intended for you to memorize at this stage, but it is good to be familiar with them from the beginning.

1. Everyday greetings

a. 안녕하세요?
    How are you?/Hello./How do you do?

Note: In Korean, 안녕하세요?, literally meaning 'Are you in peace?' is used as a greeting at any time of the day, for example, 'Good morning', 'Good afternoon', or 'Good evening'. It can also be used for 'How are you?' or 'Nice to meet you'.

b. 안녕히 계세요.
    Good-bye (to the one staying).

c. 안녕히 가세요.
    Good-bye (to the one leaving).

Note: 안녕히 계세요 literally means 'Please stay in peace', and 안녕히 가세요, 'Please go in peace'.

2. Courtesies

a.	고맙습니다.	Thank you.
	감사합니다.	Thank you.
b.	미안합니다.	I'm sorry. (to apologize)
	죄송합니다.	I'm truly sorry. (to apologize to a senior or distant equal)
	(늦어서) 죄송합니다.	I'm sorry (I am late).
c.	실례합니다.	Excuse me. (lit. I'm committing rudeness and discourtesy.)

3. Teacher's general instructions

(다같이) 따라하세요.	(All together) please repeat after me.
읽어 보세요.	Please read.
칠판을 보세요.	Please look at the blackboard.

Objectives

Lesson 1 인사 [Greetings]

Texts	Grammar
Conversation 1 저는 스티브 윌슨이에요.	1. Equational expressions: N1은/는 N2이에요/예요 2. Omission of redundant elements 3. Comparing items: 은/는 vs. 도
Conversation 2 한국 사람이에요?	4. Yes/no questions 5. Negative equational expressions: 　N1은/는 N2이/가 아니에요
Narration 한국어 클래스	

Culture	Usage
1. Greetings with a bow 2. Korean names	A. Introducing oneself B. Describing another person

Lesson 2 대학교 캠퍼스 [The University Campus]

Texts	Grammar
Conversation 1 유니온 빌딩이 어디 있어요?	1. The subject particle 이/가 2. Expressing location: [Place]에 있어요 3. Changing the topic: particle 은/는
Conversation 2 학교 식당 음식이 맛있어요.	4. Verbs vs. adjectives 5. The polite ending ~어요/아요
Narration 캠퍼스	

Culture	Usage
1. The academic calendar in 　Korea 2. Blind date	A. Inquiring about something B. Asking about the location of something or someone

Lesson 3 한국어 수업 [Korean Language Class]

Texts	Grammar
Conversation 1 오늘 수업 있으세요?	1. Expressing possession: N이/가 있어요/없어요 2. The honorific ending ~(으)세요
Conversation 2 한국어를 공부해요.	3. The object particle 을/를 4. Omission of particles
Narration 한국어 반	

Culture	Usage
Korean national symbols: 1. Korean national flag 2. Korean national flower 3. Korean national anthem	A. Inquiring about someone's well-being B. Talking about someone's major C. Describing people D. Making requests

Lesson 4 집 [At Home]

Texts	Grammar
Conversation 1 동생이 두 명 있어요.	1. Alternative questions 2. Numbers 3. Noun counters
Conversation 2 누구 방이에요?	4. Expressing possessive relations: N1(possessor) N2 (possessed) 5. Vowel contraction
Narration 내 친구 소피아	
Culture	**Usage**
1. Korean collectivism 2. 한옥과 온돌	A. Inquiring about hometown and family B. Asking and telling about quantity/counting

Lesson 5 서점에서 [At the Bookstore]

Texts	Grammar
Conversation 1 서점에서 친구를 만나요.	1. The locative particles 에 and 에서 2. The basic sentence pattern
Conversation 2 선물 사러 백화점에 가요.	3. ~으러 [place]에 가요 4. Irregular verbs in /ㄷ/
Narration 생일 선물	
Culture	**Usage**
1. 생일 미역국 (Seaweed soup for birthday)	A. Saying good-bye B. Asking and telling about destination and purpose C. Coming and going: 가다/오다

Lesson 6 나의 하루 [My Day]

Texts	Grammar
Conversation 1 차로 한 시간쯤 걸려요.	1. N(으)로 'by means of N' 2. Irregular predicates in /ㅂ/
Conversation 2 어제 뭐 했어요?	3. Past events ~었/았/ㅆ어요 4. The negative adverb 안 vs. 못
Narration 마이클의 하루	
Culture	**Usage**
1. 달력 'calendar' 2. Writing dates	A. Talking about how much time something takes B. Talking about habitual and past activities C. Talking about daily activities D. Asking reasons: 왜 'Why?'

Lesson 7 주말 [The Weekend]	
Texts	**Grammar**
Conversation 1 친구하고 영화 볼 거예요.	1. Probability: ~(으)ㄹ 거예요 2. 무슨 'what (kind of) N' vs. 어느 'which N'
Conversation 2 파티에 안 갈 거예요?	3. The clausal connective ~고 4. Negative questions
Narration 소피아의 주말	
Culture	**Usage**
1. National holidays in Korea	A. Talking about weekend plans B. Talking about likes and dislikes

Lesson 8 서울에서 [In Seoul]	
Texts	**Grammar**
Conversation 1 서울 날씨가 참 좋지요?	1. Seeking agreement: ~지요? 2. Demonstrative expressions: 이/그/저
Conversation 2 말씀 좀 묻겠습니다.	3. Deferential style ~습니다/ㅂ니다, ~습니까/ㅂ니까? 4. N(으)로 'toward N' 5. Irregular predicates in /ㄹ/
Narration 우리 동네	
Culture	**Usage**
1. Seoul 2. Getting a taxi 3. The subway system in Seoul	A. Conversing and inquiring about someone's background B. Asking and giving directions

1과 인사 [Greetings]

Conversation 1 저는 스티브 윌슨이에요.

(Students introduce themselves in a classroom.)

스티브: 안녕하세요?

저는 스티브 윌슨이에요.G1.1

3학년이에요.G1.2

유미: 안녕하세요?

저는 김유미예요.

저는G1.3 1학년이에요.

마이클: 마이클 정이에요.

저도G1.3 1학년이에요.

스티브 윌슨

김유미

마이클 정

NEW WORDS

NOUN		NUMBER	
1학년	freshman	일	① 1
2학년	sophomore	이	① 2
3학년	junior	삼	3
4학년	senior	사	4
과	lesson, chapter	**ADJECTIVE**	
대학생	college student	안녕하다(안녕하세요)	to be well
미국	the United States		('Hi'; 'Hello'; 'How
사람	person, people		are you?')
인사	greeting	**COPULA**	
학년	school year	이다 (이에요/예요)	to be (equation)
학생	student	**PARTICLE**	
한국	Korea	도	also, too
PRONOUN		은/는	topic particle
저 *hum.*	I (=나 *plain*)		('as for')

NEW EXPRESSIONS

1. 안녕하세요 is a greeting that asks about the other person's well-being or good health. This expression can be used at any time of the day. The appropriate response would be a return greeting of 안녕하세요.

2. Reference to the speaker himself/herself (first person pronoun).

	I	As for me . . .	I also . . .
Plain form	나	나는	나도
Humble form	저	저는	저도

3. In English, the given name comes first, and the family name follows it, as in "Steve Wilson." In Korean, however, as in many other Asian cultures, the family name comes first, and the given name follows it. In 저는 김유미예요, 김 is the family name, and 유미 is the given name.

4. Korean uses two sets of numbers, native Korean numbers and Sino-Korean numbers (G4.2). The following are basic Sino-Korean numbers:

0	1	2	3	4	5	6	7	8	9	10
영/공	일	이	삼	사	오	육	칠	팔	구	십

Note that the number 0 is read as 영 or 공. For telephone numbers 0 is read as 공, and in other cases it is read as 영. The telephone number 258-5037 is 이오팔(의) 오공삼칠.

Exercises

1. Fill in the blanks with appropriate words.

Michael   Sophia   Steve
freshman   sophomore   junior

(1)   마이클은 _____이에요.

(2)   소피아는 _____이에요.

(3)   스티브는 _____이에요.

2. Practice reading the following telephone numbers.

    (1)   119   (2)   370-6481

    (3)   590-2406   (4)   964-0387

    (5)   (367) 801-4592

GRAMMAR

G1.1   Equational expressions : N1은/는 N2이에요/예요

Examples

(1)   스티브 :   저는 스티브**예요**.   I'm Steve.
                 3학년**이에요**.   I'm a junior.
      유미: 김유미**예요**.   I'm Yumi Kim.
                 저는 1학년**이에요**.   I'm a freshman.

(2)   소피아 왕은 학생**이에요**.   Sophia Wang is a student.

Notes

1. Topic-comment structure

All the examples above have topic-comment structure. In Korean, topic-comment structure is the basic sentence type. Topic-comment structure is one of the fundamental ways of conveying ideas, where the speaker picks a person, an idea, or an object as the topic and contributes the subsequent statement(s) (=comments) in describing the selected item.

	Topic (N1은/는)	**Comment** (N2이에요/예요)
(i)	마이클은	대학생**이에요**.
(ii)	저는	김유미**예요**.
(iii)	–	2학년이에요.

The most typical use of topic-comment structure is in identifying statements such as the above examples, where equational expressions (N1 = N2) are used. In (i), for example, 마이클 'Michael' is the topic, and 대학생이에요 ' . . . is a college student' is the comment. In (ii), 저 'I' is the topic, and 김유미예요 ' . . . am Yumi Kim' is the comment. In (iii), the topic is omitted, because it is redundant from the preceding context (G1.2).

2. Equational expression: N1 = N2

An equational expression contains two nouns, where the first noun N1 is part of the topic, and the second noun N2 is part of the comment.

The topic particle 은/는 indicates that the attached noun is the topic described by the subsequent comment. 은 is used when the noun ends in a consonant as in 마이클은 in (i), whereas 는 is used when the noun ends in a vowel as in 저는 in (ii). When the topic contains more than one noun, the particle is attached to the last noun, as in 유미, 마이클, 스티브는 대학생이에요 'Yumi, Michael, and Steve are college students.'

The copula 이다 'to be (equation)' is attached to the second noun N2 to complete the comment structure. When N2 ends in a consonant, 이에요 (conjugated form of 이다) is used as in 대학생이에요, whereas the contracted form 예요 is used when N2 ends in a vowel as in 김유미예요.

Exercises

1. Fill in the blanks with 은 or 는.

    (1)   마이클_____ 학생이에요.

    (2)   수지('Susie')_____ 미국 사람이에요.

(3)   유미_____ 한국 사람이에요.

(4)   수잔('Susan')_____ 4학년이에요.

(5)   저_____ 1학년이에요.

2. To the given nouns, add 이에요 or 예요.

(1)   마이클: <u>저는 마이클이에요.</u>

(2)   소피아: _____

(3)   수잔: _____

(4)   제니('Jenny'): _____

(5)   리사 ('Lisa'):   _____

3. Formulate the following equational expressions in Korean.

(1)   Michael = freshman

       <u>마이클은 1학년이에요.</u>

(2)   Yumi = Korean

       _____

(3)   Steve = junior

       _____

(4)   Sophia = college student

       _____

| G1.2 | Omission of redundant elements |

Example

(1)   스티브: 안녕하세요?   How are [you]?
                 저는 스티브 윌슨이에요.   I am Steve Wilson.
                 3학년이에요.   [I] am a junior.

       유미: 안녕하세요?   How are [you]?
                 김유미예요.   [I] am Yumi Kim.

Notes

1. In Korean, subjects/topics are often omitted when they are obvious, as can be seen in the above examples.

2. Omissions are not limited to subjects. Any element can be omitted as long as the context makes the referent clear. In the above examples, not only the reference to the speaker [I] but also to the listener [you] is omitted as in 안녕하세요.

Exercise

1. Introduce yourself with your name and your year in school, as specified. Avoid redundancy as much as you can.

(1)   [스티브, 3학년, 미국 사람]
       저는 스티브예요.   3학년이에요.   미국 사람이에요.

(2)   [김유미, 1학년, 한국 사람]

       _____   _____   _____

(3)   [your own information]

       _____   _____   _____

| G1.3 | Comparing items: 은/는 vs. 도 |

Examples

(1)   김유미는 한국 사람이에요.
       스티브는 미국 사람이에요.   [different]

(2)   스티브: 안녕하세요?
                     저는 3학년이에요.
       리사: 저도 3학년이에요.   [parallel]

The particles 은/는 and 도 are used to compare two or more items:

       은/는   The items are different or contrastive.
       도   The items are parallel.

Exercise

1. Fill in the blanks with the particles 은/는 or 도.

       (1)   A: 마이클은 1학년이에요.
              B: 스티브는 3학년이에요.

(2)   A: 저는 4학년이에요.

        B: 저_____ 4학년이에요.

(3)   A: 유미는 한국 사람이에요.

        B: 제시카('Jessica')_____ 미국 사람이에요.

(4)   A: 유미는 한국 학생이에요.

        B: 마이클_____ 한국 학생이에요.

(5)   A: 스티브는 3학년이에요.

        B: 소피아_____ 2학년이에요.

CULTURE

1. Greetings with a bow

In Korea, bowing shows courtesy when you greet someone unless the other party is a junior. The degree of the bow depends on such factors as the degree of politeness, seniority, and social status. To show the highest degree of politeness, you bend your head and waist about 45°. Common courtesy to most people is shown by bending your head and waist about 15° with face downward. It is considered to be impolite to stare directly at someone (especially an older person) in Korea, while avoiding eye contact implies lack of respect or interest in Western culture.

In a very casual meeting with a person about your age, nodding your head would be enough.

Although bowing is the typical greeting in Korea, handshaking is also very common. Usually, a younger person bows first, going on to shake hands if the older person starts handshaking. The younger person often bows while shaking hands with one or both hands, unlike Western people. Most Koreans hold hands softly, not tightly. In other words, the limp handshake doesn't imply any negative impression to the other person.

Conversation 2 | 한국 사람이에요?

(Michael meets Sophia for the first time.)

마이클: 안녕하세요?

저는 마이클 정이에요.

이름이 뭐예요?

소피아: 소피아 왕이에요.

반갑습니다.

마이클   소피아

마이클: 소피아 씨는 한국 사람이에요?G1.4

소피아: 아니요, 한국 사람 아니에요.G1.5

중국 사람이에요.

마이클: 아, 그래요? 저는 한국 사람이에요.

NEW WORDS

NOUN		PARTICLE	
선생님	teacher	이/가	subject particle
씨	attached to a person's name for courtesy	**ADJECTIVE**	
		그렇다 (그래요)	to be so ('Is that right?')
영국	United Kingdom		
영어	the English language	반갑다 (반갑습니다)	to be glad ('Glad to meet you.')
이름	name		
일본	Japan	**COPULA**	
중국	China	아니다 (아니에요)	to not be (negative equation)
클래스	class		
한국어	the Korean language (=한국말)	**PRONOUN**	
ADVERB		뭐	what (=무엇)
네	① yes; ② I see; ③ okay	**INTERJECTION**	
아니요	no	아	oh

NEW EXPRESSIONS

1. The question word 뭐 'what' is a contracted form of 무엇 (무엇 > 무어 > 뭐), which is not used much in colloquial speech.

2. 이름이 뭐예요? cannot be used to a senior. To a senior, an honorific expression 성함이 어떻게 되세요? must be used.

3. 씨, as in 소피아 씨, 마이클 씨, and 김유미 씨, denotes the speaker's courtesy toward colleagues, fellow students, co-workers, or even toward his/her students, juniors, or supervisees at work. It is not appropriate to use 씨 to speak or refer to one's seniors, teachers, or older people. 씨 should be attached to the last name plus the first name (e.g., 김유미 씨) or to the first name only (e.g., 유미 씨). Attaching 씨 to Korean last names alone is condescending.

4. Korean has personal pronouns such as 저/나, but the range of pronominal expressions is much narrower than in English, and usage is very limited. In referring to the listener, which is 너 'you', pronouns are rarely used, but names and titles are used instead. For example, Michael is speaking to Sophia, and refers to her with 소피아 씨. That is, a name, 소피아, instead of a pronoun (e.g.,너 'you') , is used to refer to the listener.

5. Naming a language and nationality

Country	Language: country + 어	Nationality: country + 사람
한국 Korea	한국어	한국 사람
미국 U.S.	영어	미국 사람
영국 U.K.	영어	영국 사람
일본 Japan	일(본)어	일본 사람
중국 China	중국어	중국 사람
프랑스 France	프랑스어	프랑스 사람
스페인 Spain	스페인어	스페인 사람
러시아 Russia	러시아어	러시아 사람

6. Either 한국어 or 한국말 may be used, but the latter is usually used in colloquial speech. In addition, 한국어 may be used in complex noun phrases such as 한국어 선생님 'Korean teacher', 한국어 클래스 'Korean class', and so on.

7. The Korean word for 'English' is 영어. Note that 미국어 is a non-existent word.

Exercises

1. Look at the picture and identify each person's nationality.

| James | Michiko | Edward |

(1)   제임스는 _____이에요.
(2)   미치코는 _____이에요.
(3)   에드워드는 _____이에요.

2. Fill in the blanks with appropriate expressions.

(1)   한국 사람: 한국어   (2)   중국 사람: _____
(3)   일본 사람: _____   (4)   미국 사람: _____

3. Convert the following questions into Korean.

(1)   [to Sophia]   Are [you] a freshman?
                      소피아 씨, 1학년이에요?

(2)   [to Yumi]   Are [you] Chinese?

       _____

(3)   [to Steve]   Are [you] a sophomore?

       _____

(4)   [to Michael]   Are [you] a college student?

       _____

(5)   [to Susan]   Are [you] American?

       _____

4. Ask your partner for his/her year in school and nationality, using his/her name instead of a pronoun.

GRAMMAR

G1.4 Yes/no questions

Examples

(1)   마이클: 유미 씨, 한국 사람이에요?
       유미: **네**, 한국 사람이에요.

(2)   스티브: 소피아 씨, 3학년이에요?
       소피아: **아니요**, 2학년이에요.

Notes

1. In English, a question involves special grammar. Namely, a verb (either 'do' or 'be') is placed before the subject, as in

   Are you Korean? (compare with 'You are Korean.')

   In Korean, however, only the intonations change (e.g., rising intonation), and no special grammar is used, at least in the polite (G2.5) and intimate speech styles. The word order remains the same, and the same verbal ending is used both for questions and for statements. That is, the equational construction N이에요/예요 can be made into a question merely by changing the intonation.

2. Answering a yes/no question involves affirmation or denial of the content of the question. In Korean, an affirmative answer is made with 네(예 is an alternative form), indicating that the content of the question is true, and a denial is made with 아니요, which indicates that the content of the question is false.

Answering a yes/no question: Content is true   네
                                Content is not true   아니요

Exercises

1. Say 네 or 아니요, whichever is appropriate for the given context.

(1)   A: 일본 사람이에요?
       B: 아니요, 중국 사람이에요.

(2)   A: 3학년이에요?
       B: _____, 1학년이에요.

(3)   A: 미국 사람이에요?

      B: _____, 미국 사람이에요.

(4)   A: 선생님이에요?

      B: _____, 학생이에요.

(5)   A: 한국어 선생님이에요?

      B: _____, 영어 선생님이에요.

2. Make up a question that will lead to the answer given.

(1)   A: <u>대학생이에요</u>?

      B: 네, 대학생이에요.

(2)   A: _____?

      B: 네, 영국 사람이에요.

(3)   A: _____?

      B: 아니요, 한국어 선생님이에요.

(4)   A: _____?

      B: 네, 4학년이에요.

(5)   A: _____?

      B: 아니요, 한국어 클래스예요.

G1.5 Negative equational expressions: N1은/는 N2이/가 아니에요

Examples

(1)   소피아 왕은 선생님**이 아니에요**.
      학생이에요.

(2)   유미: 스티브 씨, 1학년이에요?
      스티브: 아니요, 1학년 **아니에요**.
                 3학년이에요.

(3)   소피아 왕**은** 일본 사람**이 아니에요**. 중국 사람이에요.
      스티브 윌슨**도** 일본 사람**이 아니에요**. 미국 사람이에요.

Notes

1. The negative counterpart of [N1은/는 N2이에요/예요] is [N1은/는 N2이/가
아니에요], where N2 is followed by the particle 이/가 (G2.1). The particle 이 is
used when the N2 ends in a consonant, or 가 when it ends in a vowel.

N1은	N2이 아니에요	N1는	N2가 아니에요
소피아 왕은	1학년**이** 아니에요.	저는	스티브**가** 아니에요.
	한국 사람**이** 아니에요.		제니**가** 아니에요.

2. As illustrated in example (3), the particle 도 'also' (G1.3) is used in negative
sentences as long as the sentence containing it is parallel with the previous
sentence.

3. In conversation, the particle 이/가 is often omitted (G3.4).

Exercise

1. To the given nouns, add (i) 이에요/예요 and (ii) 이/가 아니에요.

    (1)   마이클/한국 사람: 마이클은 한국 사람이에요.
                                     마이클은 한국 사람이 아니에요.

    (2)   스티브/2학년: _____

_____

    (3)   저/제니: _____

_____

    (4)   유미/학생: _____

_____

    (5)   저/린다: _____

_____

    (6)   선생님/영국 사람: _____

_____

Narration 한국어 클래스

이민수 선생님은 한국어 선생님이에요. 한국 사람이에요.
김유미, 마이클 정, 소피아 왕, 스티브 윌슨은 한국어 클래스
학생이에요. 김유미는 한국 사람이에요. 마이클 정도 한국 사람
이에요. 소피아 왕은 한국 사람이 아니에요. 중국 사람이에요.
스티브 윌슨도 한국 사람이 아니에요. 미국 사람이에요.

이민수 선생님   김유미   마이클 정   소피아 왕   스티브 윌슨

Exercises

1. Fill in the blanks based on the narration.

    (1)   이민수 선생님은 _____ 선생님이에요.

    (2)   김유미는 한국어 클래스 _____이에요.

    (3)   스티브 윌슨도 _____이에요.

    (4)   마이클 정은 _____이에요.

    (5)   소피아 왕은 한국 사람이 아니에요. _____이에요.

2. Fill in the blanks with the appropriate particles provided below:

이/가	은/는	도

이민수 선생님_____ 한국어 선생님이에요. 한국 사람이에요. 김유미, 마이클 정, 소피아 왕, 스티브 윌슨_____ 한국어 클래스 학생이에요. 김유미_____ 한국 사람이에요. 마이클 정_____ 한국 사람이에요. 소피아 왕_____ 한국 사람_____ 아니에요. 중국 사람이에요. 스티브 윌슨_____ 한국 사람이 아니에요. 미국 사람이에요.

3. Fill in the blanks with 이에요/예요 or 아니에요.

안녕하세요? 저는 김유미_____. 저는 한국 사람_____. 한국어 클래스 학생_____. 이민수 선생님은 한국어 선생님_____. 한국 사람_____. 마이클 정, 소피아 왕, 스티브 윌슨은 한국어 클래스 학생_____. 마이클 정은 한국 사람_____. 소피아 왕은 한국 사람이 _____. 중국 사람_____. 스티브 윌슨도 한국 사람이 _____. 미국 사람_____.

CULTURE

2. Korean names

In Korean, as in many other Asian cultures, the family name comes first, and the given name follows. Most Korean names consist of three Sino-Korean characters: the first single character is the family name and the following two characters the given name, although a few family names such as 남궁 and 황보 have two characters and a few given names have a single character. Korean names have no middle names. In 김유미, 김 is the family name, and 유미 is the given name.

Throughout this textbook, we will follow the customs of each language in presenting names. That is, Korean names will be presented in the Korean way, e.g., 김유미, and English names will be presented in the English way, e.g., 스티브 윌슨 (Steve Wilson).

Korean family names have more significance than their English counterparts in that they represent kin that may be traced back hundreds of years. There are 259 last names reported in Korea. The five most common last names are 김, 이, 박, 최, and 정. Usually romanized as Kim in English, 김 is the most common (21.7%), followed by 이, commonly spelled as Lee, Rhee, or Yi, and 박, as Park, Pak, or Bak. Another important thing to note in Korean names is that Korean women do not take the surnames or their husbands.

USAGE

A. Introducing oneself

[Exercise 1] Introduce yourself as in the example below. Include your (i) name, (ii) school year, and (iii) nationality.

> 안녕하세요? 저는 (i) 마이클 정이에요.
> (ii) 1학년이에요. (iii) 한국 사람이에요.

[Exercise 2] Based on the following summary, introduce yourself as if you were the person specified.

Name	School year	Nationality
스티브 윌슨	junior	American
김유미	freshman	Korean
미치코 카노	senior	Japanese
소피아 왕	sophomore	Chinese

B. Describing another person

You: 이름이 뭐예요?   ← Asking name
마이클: 마이클 정이에요.

You: 2학년이에요?   ← Asking school year
마이클: 아니요, 1학년이에요.

You: 한국 사람이에요?   ← Asking nationality
마이클: 네, 한국 사람이에요.

Use [N이에요/예요?] to obtain the necessary information about the other party. Having obtained the information, you can describe him or her to the rest of the class.

> 마이클 정은 1학년이에요.
> 마이클 정은 미국 사람이 아니에요.
> 한국 사람이에요.

[Exercise 1] Describe the main characters in lesson 1 in Korean. Use appropriate particles (e.g., 이/가, 은/는, 도) as needed.

(1)　　　이민수 선생님

(2)　　　스티브 윌슨

(3)　　　김유미

(4)　　　소피아 왕

(5)　　　마이클 정

[Exercise 2] Interview three people in the class and fill in the table, then introduce your interviewees to the rest of the class.

Name	School year	Nationality
스티브 윌슨	3학년	미국 사람

Lesson 1 Greetings

CONVERSATION 1: I'm Steve Wilson.
(Students introduce themselves in a classroom.)

Steve:	Hello. I'm Steve Wilson. I'm a junior.
Yumi:	Hi. I'm Yumi Kim. I'm a freshman.
Michael:	I'm Michael Jung. I'm also a freshman.

CONVERSATION 2: Are you Korean?
(Michael meets Sophia for the first time.)

Michael:	Hello. I'm Michael Jung. What is your name?
Sophia:	I'm Sophia Wang. Glad to meet you.
Michael:	Are you Korean?
Sophia:	No, I'm not Korean. I'm Chinese.
Michael:	Oh, really? I'm Korean.

NARRATION: Korean class

Professor Minsoo Lee is the instructor of the Korean class. He is Korean. Yumi Kim, Michael Jung, Sophia Wang, and Steve Wilson are his students. Yumi Kim is Korean. Michael Chung is also Korean. Sophia Wang is not Korean. Sophia is Chinese. Steve Wilson isn't Korean either. Steve is American.

2과 대학 캠퍼스 [The University Campus]

Conversation 1	유니온 빌딩이 어디 있어요?

(Yumi is looking for the school cafeteria and runs into Lisa.)

리사   유미

유미: 저어, 학교 식당이[G2.1] 어디 있어요?

리사: 유니온 빌딩 3층에 있어요.[G2.2]

          도서관 뒤에도 있어요.

유미: 유니온 빌딩은[G2.3] 어디 있어요?

리사: 우체국 앞에 있어요.

NEW WORDS

NOUN			
		의자	chair
가방	bag	책	book
기숙사	dormitory	책방	bookstore
대학교	college, university	책상	desk
도서관	library	캠퍼스	campus
유니온 빌딩	Union Building	학교	school
시계	clock, watch	학생회관	student center
식당	restaurant (학교 식당 'school cafeteria')	**COUNTER**	
		층	floor, layer (1층, 2층, 3층 . . .)
안	the inside		
앞	the front	**ADJECTIVE**	
뒤	the back, behind	있다(있어요)	① to be (existence)
옆	the side, beside	**INTERJECTION**	
어디	what place, where (question word)	저어	uh (expression of hesitation)
우체국	post office	**PARTICLE**	
위	the top side, above	에	① in, at, on (indicates a static location)
밑	the bottom, below		

NEW EXPRESSIONS

1. 저어 is an expression used for hesitation before the speaker says something. The hesitation draws the attention of the listener.

2. 이에요/예요 vs. 있어요
In English, the copula 'to be' can be used for both (i) equation or identification and (ii) a statement of existence.

> (i) Equation/identification: My major is economics.
> (ii) Existence of an entity: The cafeteria is in the Union Building.

In Korean, two different verbs are used; (i)이다 'to be (equation)', and (ii)있다 'to be (existence)'. 이다 cannot be used for existence, and 있다 cannot be used for equation/identification.

Correct:	저는 학생**이에요.**	I am a student.
Incorrect:	저는 학생 있어요.	
Correct:	학교 식당은 유니온 빌딩에 **있어요.**	The school cafeteria is in the Union Building.
Incorrect:	학교 식당은 유니온 빌딩이에요.	

Exercises

1. Fill in the blanks with 위, 밑, 옆, 앞, 뒤, or 안.

      (1)   한국은 중국 <u>옆</u> 에 있어요.

      (2)   캐나다'Canada'는 미국 _____에 있어요.

      (3)   멕시코'Mexico'는 미국 _____에 있어요.

      (4)   멕시코는 쿠바'Cuba' _____에 있어요.

2. List things or places you can find from your own university campus.

      도서관, _____, _____, _____,_____, _____.

GRAMMAR

| G2.1 | The subject particle 이/가 |

Examples

(1)   A: 이름**이** 뭐예요?
        B: 스티브 윌슨이에요.

(2)   A: 학교 식당**이** 어디 있어요?
        B: 학생회관에 있어요.

(3)   시계**가** 책상 위에 있어요.

Notes

1. The particle 이/가 indicates that the word attached to it is the subject of the sentence, that is, what the predicate is about. The particle 이 is used when the subject noun ends in a consonant, whereas 가 is used when the subject noun ends in a vowel.

Subject	Predicate
도서관**이**	유니온 빌딩에 있어요.
기숙사**가**	

2. 이/가 usually but not always marks the subject. In the following example the noun used with 이/가 is not the subject (G1.5).

소피아 왕은 일본 사람**이** 아니에요.

3. Note that the first person pronoun 나/저 become 내/제 when the subject particle 가 is attached.

Plain form	나	나는	나도	내가
Humble form	저	저는	저도	제가

Exercises

1. Fill in the blanks with the subject particle 이/가.

    (1)   A: 유미_____ 도서관에 있어요?

              B: 아니요, 기숙사에 있어요.

    (2)   A: 이름_____ 뭐예요?

              B: 리사예요.

    (3)   A: 수지 씨, 도서관_____ 어디 있어요?

              B: 유니온 빌딩 옆에 있어요.

2. Fill in the blanks with the appropriate particles: 이/가, 은/는, or 도.

    (1)   A: 이름이 뭐예요?

              B: 김유미예요.

    (2)   A: 소피아 씨, 2학년이에요?

              B: 네, 2학년이에요. 리사 씨_____ 2학년이에요?

              A: 아니요. 저_____ 2학년이에요.

    (3)   A: 저어, 학교 식당_____ 어디 있어요?

              B: 유니온 빌딩에 있어요.

              A: 기숙사_____ 어디 있어요?

              B: 도서관 뒤에 있어요.

G2.2   Expressing location: [Place]에 있어요

Examples

(1)   A: 책방이 어디 **있어요?**
      B: 우체국 옆에 **있어요.**

(2)   학교 식당은 유니온 빌딩 안에 **있어요.**
      도서관 밑에도 학교 식당이 **있어요.**

(3)   기숙사 앞에는 도서관이 **있어요.**
      기숙사 뒤에는 학생회관이 **있어요.**

Notes

1. Reference to a location of an entity requires three elements in Korean:
   - (a)   a location
   - (b)   a locative particle 에
   - (c)   a verb of existence 있다(있어요)

Entity	Location	Locative particle	Verb of existence
학교 식당이	유니온 빌딩	에	있어요.
소피아가	책방		

   Sometimes a reference to a location needs to be further specified with a "position-noun" indicating front, back, side, inside, under, or above.

Entity	Location		Locative particle	Verb of existence
	Relative location	Relative position		
유니온 빌딩은	우체국	앞 (front)	에	있어요.
학생회관은	유니온 빌딩	뒤 (behind)	에	있어요.
가방은	의자	옆 (beside)	에	있어요.
학교 식당은	유니온 빌딩	안 (inside)	에	있어요.
	도서관	밑 (below)	에도	있어요.
책은	책상	위 (above)	에	있어요.

2. In referring to the location of an object/person, the locative particle 에 and the existential verb 있다 (있어요), not 이다 (이에요/예요), must be used.

In English, locations are expressed usually by prepositions such as 'on', 'above', 'in', 'under', 'below', 'beside', and 'behind', followed by a relative location (e.g., a library). In Korean, locations are expressed by a sequence of a relative location (e.g., 도서관), the noun indicating the relative position (e.g., 뒤 'back'), and the locative particle 에 'in, at': 도서관 뒤에 'behind the library', 도서관 위에 'above the library', and 도서관 옆에 'beside the library'.

3. In asking for the location of something, the question word 어디 is used, like 'where' in English. Unlike in English, where question words are placed at the beginning of a sentence, 어디 is placed immediately before the verb 있어요. In conversation, the particle 에 is often omitted after 어디.

A:	우체국이 어디 있어요?	Where is the post office?
B:	학생회관 안에 있어요.	It's in the student center.

4. In some cases, the particles 은/는 and 도 can be added even after another particle such as 에 'in, at, on' as in 학교 식당은 도서관 밑에도 있어요. However, it should be noted that subject particle 이/가 cannot be added to 에.

5. Korean allows reordering of the nominal elements within the same sentence. In example (2), for instance, 도서관 밑에도 학교 식당이 있어요 and 학교 식당이 도서관 밑에도 있어요 have the same meaning with only slight connotative difference in terms of focus.

Exercises

1. Answer the questions, based on the following picture.

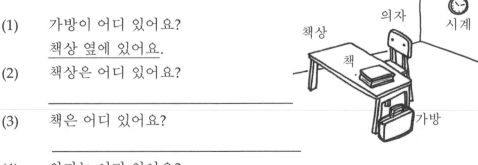

(1) 가방이 어디 있어요?
     책상 옆에 있어요.

(2) 책상은 어디 있어요?
     _____

(3) 책은 어디 있어요?
     _____

(4) 의자는 어디 있어요?
     _____

(5) 시계는 어디 있어요?
     _____

2. Based on the following picture, give the location of the buildings named in the questions.

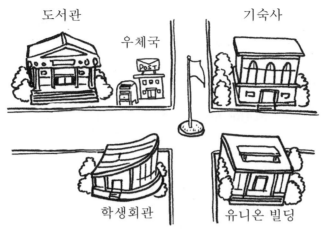

도서관   우체국   기숙사

학생회관   유니온 빌딩

(1)   A: 유니온 빌딩이 어디 있어요?

        B: 기숙사 <u>앞에</u> 있어요.

(2)   A: 우체국이 어디 있어요?

        B: 학생회관 _____ 있어요.

(3)   A: 도서관이 어디 있어요?

        B: 우체국 _____ 있어요.

(4)   A: 학생회관이 어디 있어요?

        B: 우체국 _____ 있어요.

(5)   A: 기숙사가 어디 있어요?

        B: 유니온 빌딩 _____ 있어요.

G2.3   Changing the topic: particle 은/는

Examples

(1)   유미: 저어, 학교 식당이 어디 있어요?
       리사: 유니온 빌딩 1층에 있어요.
       유미: 유니온 빌딩**은** 어디 있어요?
       리사: 학생회관 앞에 있어요.

(2)   스티브: 우체국이 어디 있어요?   Where is the post office?
       마이클: 도서관 뒤에 있어요.   It's behind the library.

       스티브: 책방**은**요?   How about the bookstore?
       마이클: 학생회관 안에 있어요.   It's in the student center.

Notes

1. Recall that the particle 은/는 is used to mark a topic of a sentence (G1.1), or a contrast between two items in comparison (G1.3). This use can be extended to shifting the topic from one item to another so that the speaker signals that he or she is now going on to something different.

   In example (1), 유미 and 리사 initially talk about the location of 학교 식당. 유미 wants to know about the location of 유니온 빌딩 mentioned in 리사's response. This shift of topic is signaled by the topic particle 은 attached to 유니온 빌딩 in 유미's second question.

2. ~은요/는요?—best translated as 'What about . . .?' or 'How about . . .?'—is used to request the listener to focus on a different item, as in 책방은요? in example (2). Note that the predicate 어디 있어요? is omitted from 스티브's second question, leaving only the topic 책방은요?

Exercise

1. Use the particle 은 or 는 to change the topic.

   (1)   A: 가방이 어디 있어요?
          B: 의자 옆에 있어요.
          A: 의자는 어디 있어요?
          B: 책상 뒤에 있어요.

   (2)   A: 도서관이 어디 있어요?
          B: 우체국 옆에 있어요.
          A: 기숙사_____?
          B: 학생회관 뒤에 있어요.

   (3)   A: 학교 식당이 유니온 빌딩 안에 있어요?
          B: 네, 1층에 있어요.
          A: 책방_____?
          B: 유니온 빌딩 2층에 있어요.

CULTURE

1. The academic calendar in Korea

In Korea, the school year is divided into two terms. The first semester (1학기 or 봄 학기) starts in early March and lasts until mid-July. Then there is summer vacation (여름 방학) for about a month. The second semester (2학기 or 가을 학기) usually resumes in late August and runs until late February, with a long winter break (겨울 방학) from mid-December to early February. Korean students were required to go to school every day except Sunday, but as the nation incrementally introduced a five-day work schedule, schools have been adjusting to the new system since 2005. Elementary and secondary school students go to school on Saturday every other week as of 2006. In recent years, a few colleges and universities have begun to offer classes on Saturday.

2. Blind dates

Education is seen as the most important key to success in Korea, and competition is very heated and fierce. Thus, entrance into a prestigious college is the focus of intense energy and dedication in high school. Students are often studying too hard, or they may be attending segregated high schools, so dating is not that common among Korean high school students. Thus, many Koreans have the opportunity to date only during their college years or after graduating high school. Typically, a big group of friends goes out together to socialize; this gathering is called 미팅. Sometimes, parents or friends set up a blind date. The blind dates are called '맞선' or '소개팅'. People often live with their parents until marriage.

Conversation 2 | 학교 식당 음식이 맛있어요.

(Lisa is eating breakfast in the school cafeteria. Steve enters the cafeteria and sees her.)

스티브: 안녕하세요, 리사 씨?

리사: 어, 스티브 씨.

스티브: 뭐 해요?G2.4

리사: 아침 먹어요.G2.5

스티브: 학교 식당 음식이 어때요?

리사: 좋아요. 그리고 아주 싸요.

스티브: 커피도 괜찮아요?

리사: 네, 맛있어요.

NEW WORDS

NOUN		ADVERB	
숙제(하다)	homework	아주	very, really
아침	① breakfast;	참	① really, truly
	② morning	**VERB**	
음식	food	가다	to go
커피	coffee	먹다(먹어요)	to eat
ADJECTIVE		앉다	to sit
괜찮다(괜찮아요)	to be all right, okay	알다	to know
넓다	to be spacious, wide	하다(해요)	to do
많다	to be many, much	**INTERJECTION**	
맛있다(맛있어요)	to be delicious	어	oh
싸다(싸요)	to be cheap	**SUFFIX**	
어떻다(어때요)	to be how	~어요/아요	polite ending
좋다(좋아요)	to be good, nice	**CONJUNCTION**	
크다	to be big	그리고	and

NEW EXPRESSIONS

1. 어때요? is an expression asking the other party's opinion, that is, 'How is
_____?' Note that [어떻 + 어요 = 어때요].

음식이 어때요?   How's the food?
학교가 어때요?   How's school?

2. 괜찮아요 means that the situation is positive, not disturbing or displeasing.
Depending on the situation, it could mean 'It's OK' or 'It's not bad'.

3. The question word 뭐 'what' is frequently used in the following questions.

(a) 이름이 뭐예요?   What is the (or your) name?
(b) 전화 번호가 뭐예요?   What is the (or your) phone number?
                          (전화 'telephone'; 번호 'number')
(c) 이게 뭐예요?   What is this?
    이게 is a contraction of [이것 'this thing' + 이 (subject particle)]
(d) 뭐 해요?   What do you do? / What are you doing?

4. 그리고 is a conjunction that means 'and'. It usually connects two sentences.

대학 캠퍼스가 넓어요. 그리고 학생이 많아요.

Exercises

1. Fill in the blanks based on conversation 2.

      (1)   스티브는 _____에 있어요.

      (2)   리사는 _____ 먹어요.

      (3)   학교 식당 _____이 맛있어요.

      (4)   학교 식당 _____도 괜찮아요.

2. Answer the following questions.

      (1)   대학교 캠퍼스가 어때요?   <u>커요.</u>

      (2)   기숙사 음식이 어때요?   _____

      (3)   한국어 클래스가 어때요?   _____

      (4)   학교 식당 커피가 어때요?   _____

      (5)   도서관이 어때요?   _____

3. Complete the sentences using 그리고 'and'.

      (1)   캠퍼스 안에 책방이 있어요. <u>그리고 우체국도 있어요.</u>

      (2)   유니온 빌딩에 도서관이 있어요. _____

      (3)   학교 식당 음식이 참 싸요. _____

      (4)   저는 대학생이에요. _____

GRAMMAR

G2.4   Verbs vs. adjectives

Predicate expressions in Korean can largely be classified into two groups, verbs and adjectives. Verbs typically denote actions and processes (including mental processes), whereas adjectives typically denote states (size, weight, quality, quantity, shape, appearance, perception, and emotion). The distinction is very important in Korean grammar, and this will become clearer in later lessons. Compare some of the verbs and adjectives that appear in this lesson.

Verbs		Adjectives	
가요	go	괜찮아요	be all right
먹어요	eat	많아요	be many, much
숙제해요	do homework	맛있어요	be delicious
앉아요	sit	좋아요	be good
알아요	know	커요	be big, large

1. Notice that while adjectives in English need the copula 'to be' in order to be used as predicates (e.g., It is cheap), adjectives in Korean are used directly as predicates without the copula 이에요/예요: 싸요 not 싸이요.

> 책이 싸요.　　　vs.　　　The book <u>is cheap</u>.

2. 있어요 'to be, exist' is a verb/adjective of existence. It behaves like a verb in some places and like an adjective in others.

3. The copula 이에요/예요 'to be (equation)' (G1.1) is a special kind of adjective which expresses an equational relation, like 'to be' in English.

Exercise

1. Based on the meaning of the predicate given, identify whether it is a verb (V) or an adjective (A).

(1)	먹어요	<u>　V　</u>		(2)	가요	_____
(3)	커요	_____		(4)	괜찮아요	_____
(5)	앉아요	_____		(6)	맛있어요	_____
(7)	넓어요	_____		(8)	알아요	_____
(9)	많아요	_____		(10)	싸요	_____
(11)	숙제해요	_____		(12)	좋아요	_____

| G2.5 | The polite ending ~어요/아요 |

Examples

(1)   유미: 시계가 어디 있어요?
       리사: 책상 위에 있어요.

(2)   유미: 학교 식당 음식이 어때요?
       리사: 맛있어요. 그리고 참 싸요.

Notes

1. The structure of predicates consists of a stem and an ending. For dictionary entries, the meaningless ending ~다 is attached to verb and adjective stems. Examples of dictionary forms are given below.

Copula stem	Ending		Verb stem	Ending		Adjective stem	Ending
이	다		하	다		맛있	다
아니	다		먹	다		괜찮	다
			앉	다		좋	다

2. The polite ending ~어요/아요 is the most frequently used form in conversation. It has a number of variations. The lefthand column in each of the following boxes gives verb/adjective stems. In the righthand column, the first row gives the dictionary ending ~다, and the second row the appropriate polite ending ~어요/아요.

(a) When the last vowel of the stem is either 아 or 오, ~아요 is used.

좋	다 'to be good'
	아요

앉	다 'to sit (down)'
	아요

(b) All other stems take ~어요.

먹	다 'to eat'
	어요

있	다 'to exist'
	어요

(c) There are exceptions to the above rules.

이	다 'to be'
	에요(or 예요)

아니	다 'to not be'
	에요

하다 'to do'
해요

All verbs/adjectives that contain 하다 'to do' are subject to this change.

숙제하다 'to do homework'
숙제해요

(d) Vowel contractions may change the ending.

가	다 'to go'
	요 (가+~아요)

싸	다 'to be cheap'
	요 (싸+~아요)

크다 'to be big'
커요 (크+~어요)

Exercises

1. Given the dictionary forms, write the polite forms using ~어요 or ~아요.

(1)	먹다	먹어요	(2)	숙제하다	_____
(3)	크다	_____	(4)	있다	_____
(5)	앉다	_____	(6)	맛있다	_____
(7)	싸다	_____	(8)	가다	_____
(9)	좋다	_____	(10)	많다	_____

2. Given the polite forms, write the dictionary forms.

(1)	먹어요	먹다	(2)	이에요/예요	_____
(3)	넓어요	_____	(4)	괜찮아요	_____
(5)	숙제해요	_____	(6)	아니에요	_____
(7)	앉아요	_____	(8)	커요	_____

Narration | 캠퍼스

대학교 캠퍼스는 참 넓어요. 그리고 학생이 많아요. 도서관도
아주 커요. 학교 식당은 유니온 빌딩 안에 있어요. 음식이 싸요.
그리고 커피가 맛있어요. 유니온 빌딩 안에는 책방도 있어요.
유니온 빌딩 뒤에는 학생회관이 있어요. 학생회관이 아주
좋아요.

Exercises

1. Answer the questions based on the narration.

     (1)   학교 식당은 어디 있어요?

     (2)   책방은 어디 있어요?

     (3)   학생회관은 어디 있어요?

     (4)   학교 식당 음식은 어때요?

     (5)   도서관은 어때요?

2. Change the dictionary forms in parentheses into the polite form ~어요 or ~아요.

대학교 캠퍼스는 참 _____(넓다). 그리고 학생이 _____ (많다).
도서관도 아주_____(크다). 학교 식당은 유니온 빌딩 안에_____
(있다). 음식이_____ (싸다). 그리고 커피가_____ (맛있다).
유니온 빌딩 안에는 책방도_____ (있다). 유니온 빌딩 뒤에는
학생회관이_____ (있다). 학생회관이 아주_____ (좋다).

USAGE

A. Inquiring about something

유미:　　　　　마이클 씨, 학교 식당 커피가 어때요?
마이클:　　　　맛있어요.

[Exercise] Create questions that could probe the following adjectives.

좋다 / 맛있다 / 괜찮다 / 싸다 / 크다 / 넓다

B. Asking about the location of something or someone

You can use the pattern below for asking about and giving the location of people, objects, or places.

(1)　A:　마이클이 어디 있어요?　　　　Where's Michael?
　　　B:　학교에 있어요.　　　　　　　He's at school.

(2)　A:　책이 어디 있어요?　　　　　　Where's the book?
　　　B:　가방 안에 있어요.　　　　　　It's in the bag.

[Exercise 1] Ask for and give the location of places on your campus using 위, 밑, 옆, 앞, 뒤, or 안.

(1)　　[학교 식당]　　A:　학교 식당이 어디 있어요?
　　　　　　　　　　　B:　학교 식당은 유니온 빌딩 안에 있어요.
(2)　　[도서관]　　　A:　_____?
　　　　　　　　　　　B:　_____

(3)   [기숙사]   A: _____?

              B: _____

(4)   [책방]   A: _____?

              B: _____

(5)   [학생회관]   A: _____?

              B: _____

(6)   [우체국]   A: _____?

              B: _____

[Exercise 2] Answer the questions by specifying the relative position of the person in question with respect to the one given in [ ].

(1)   리사가 어디 있어요?

       [유미] 유미 앞에 있어요.

(2)   소피아는 어디 있어요?

       [스티브] _____

(3)   마이클은 어디 있어요?

       [스티브] _____

(4)   유미는 어디 있어요?

       [스티브] _____

(5)   스티브는 어디 있어요?

       [마이클] _____

Lesson 2 The University Campus

CONVERSATION 1: Where is the Union Building?
(Yumi is looking for the school cafeteria and runs into Lisa.)

Yumi: Uh, where is the cafeteria?
Lisa: It's on the third floor of the Union Building. There is one behind
               the library, too.
Yumi: Where is the Union Building?
Lisa: It's in front of the post office.

CONVERSATION 2: The food at the school cafeteria is delicious.
(Lisa is eating breakfast in the school cafeteria. Steve enters the cafeteria and sees
her.)

Steve: Hi, Lisa.
Lisa: Oh, Steve.
Steve: What are you doing?
Lisa: I'm eating breakfast.
Steve: How is the food at the school cafeteria?
Lisa: It's good and pretty cheap.
Steve: Is the coffee okay, too?
Lisa: Yes, it's delicious

NARRATION: Campus

The university campus is quite extensive, and there are many students. The
library is very big. The school cafeteria is inside the Union Building. The food
is affordable and the coffee is good. There is also a bookstore inside the Union
Building. There is a student center behind the Union Building. The student center
is very nice.

3과 한국어 수업 [Korean Language Class]

Conversation 1 | 오늘 수업 있으세요?

제니: 마이클 씨, 오늘 수업 있으세요?[G3.1]

마이클: 네, 한국어 수업이 있어요. 제니 씨는요?

제니: 오늘은 수업이 없어요.
그런데, 내일은 경제학 수업이 있어요.
한국어 수업은 재미있어요?

마이클: 네, 아주 재미있어요. 그리고 선생님도 좋으세요.[G3.2]

제니: 선생님이 누구세요?

마이클: 이민수 선생님이세요.

제니: 한국어 반에 학생이 많아요?

마이클: 네, 많아요.

NEW WORDS

NOUN		PRONOUN	
경제학	economics	누구	who (누구+가=누가)
교과서	textbook	**VERB**	
교실	classroom	인사하다	to greet
내일	tomorrow	읽다	to read
반	class	**ADJECTIVE**	
사전	dictionary	없다(없어요)	① to not be (existence);
수업	course, class		② to not have
시간	① time	있다(있어요)	② to have
여자	woman	재미있다(재미있어요)	to be interesting, fun
오늘	today	**CONJUNCTION**	
우산	umbrella	그런데	① but, however
질문	question	**SUFFIX**	
집	home, house	~(으)세요	honorific polite ending
친구	friend		
컴퓨터	computer		

NEW EXPRESSIONS

1. Referring to days:

어제	오늘	내일
yesterday	today	tomorrow

2. 은요/는요? in '제니 씨는요?'—best translated as 'What about . . .?' or 'How about . . .?'—is used to request the listener to focus on a different item (G2.3).

3. When 누구 'who' is attached to the subject particle 가, 누가 should be used instead of 누구가.

A:	리사가 **누구**예요?	Who is Lisa?
B:	리사는 **마이클 여자 친구**예요.	She's Michael's girlfriend.
A:	**누가** 학교에 있어요?	Who is at the school?
B:	**유미가** 학교에 있어요.	Yumi is at the school.

4. 그런데 'but' is a frequently used conjunction that connects two sentences as in the following examples.

기숙사가 넓어요. 그런데 아주 싸요.
오늘은 수업이 없어요. 그런데 내일은 수업이 많아요.

Exercises

1. Ask your classmates whether they have the following items.

> A: _____씨, <u>가방</u> 있어요?
> B: 네, 있어요/아니요, 없어요.

2. Complete the dialogues using 그런데 'but, however'.

> (1)   소피아: 한국어 수업 재미있어요?
>   마이클: 네, 재미있어요.
>   그런데 _____
> (2)   스티브: 리사 씨, 오늘 한국어 숙제 있어요?
>   리사: 아니요, 없어요.
>   그런데 _____
> (3)   유미: 학교 식당 음식이 어때요?
>   제니: 괜찮아요. 커피도 맛있어요.
>   그런데 _____

GRAMMAR

G3.1   Expressing possession: N이/가 있어요/없어요

Examples

(1) 선생님: 유미 씨, 한국어 사전 **있어요?**   Yumi, do you have a Korean
                                                   dictionary?

     유미: 네, **있어요.**   Yes, I have one.
              그런데 집에 있어요.   But it is at home.

(2) 선생님: 질문 **있어요?**   Do you have any questions?
     리사: 아니요, **없어요.**   No, I don't.

(3) 오늘 한국어 수업이 **있어요.**   I have a Korean class today.

Notes

1. 있다 refers to either existence or possession of an object or person. Its opposite meaning, non-existence or non-possession, is expressed by 없다.

2. The meaning of 있다 (있어요) in example (1) is possession. When used as 'to have/to not have', 있다/없다 are usually preceded by [N이/가]. The particle 이/가 is often omitted in spoken form (G3.4).

> [possession]
> 질문이 있어요.   I have a question.
> 영어 사전이 없어요.   I don't have any English dictionary.

3. The meaning of 있다 is existence (G2.2) in 집에 있어요 in example (1). When used as 'to be/to not be (existence)', 있다/없다 are preceded by [place]에.

> [existence]
> 책방이 어디 있어요?   Where is the bookstore?
> 학생회관에 있어요.   It is in the student center.

Exercises

1. Create short dialogues using the words in brackets.

(1)	[한국어 교과서]	A:	한국어 교과서 있어요?
		B:	네, 있어요.
(2)	[우산]	A:	_____?
		B:	네, _____
(3)	[여자 친구]	A:	_____?
		B:	아니요,_____
(4)	[시간]	A:	내일 _____?
		B:	아니요,_____
(5)	[숙제]	A:	오늘 _____?
		B:	네, _____

2. Translate the following sentences into Korean.

(1) I have a computer class today.

(2) Steve does not have a watch.

(3)   Lisa is in the classroom.

(4)   The teacher has a Korean textbook.

G3.2   The honorific ending ~(으)세요

Examples

(1)   제니: 선생님, 우산 **있으세요?**   Do you have an umbrella?
       선생님: 아니요, 없어요.   No, I don't.

(2)   (Sophia and Lisa are talking about Professor Lee.)

       소피아: 한국어 반 선생님이 **누구세요?**   Who is the instructor for
                                          Korean class?
       리사: 이민수 **선생님이세요.**   It's Professor Minsoo Lee.

(3)   스티브 씨, **앉으세요.**   Steve, please have a seat.

Notes

1. The suffix ~(으)세요 is an honorific form of ~어요/아요. It is a combination of the honorific marker ~(으)시 and the polite ending ~어요, that is, [~(으)시 + 어요 = ~(으)세요].

~으세요 (after a consonant)		~세요 (after a vowel)	
좋	으세요	크	세요
앉	으세요	가	세요
읽	으세요	인사하	세요

2. When addressing a listener to whom you show respect, ~(으)세요 is used. In example (1), 제니 asks a professor if he has an umbrella, and uses the ~(으)세요 ending, showing her respect for the professor. In response, the professor uses the non-honorific ~어요/아요, because the person being talked about or the listener is an equal or an inferior. In this case, ~(으)세요 is not used.

3. ~(으)세요 is used when the speaker respects the person being talked about. Professor Lee is respected by both Sophia and Lisa, so in talking about him, they use ~(으)세요 in example (2).

4. Requesting an action typically takes ~(으)세요 to show respect for the listener, as in 앉으세요 in example (3) as well as in the following examples.

Dictionary form	~어요/아요	~(으)세요	
가다	가요	가세요	Please go.
앉다	앉아요	앉으세요	Please sit.
인사하다	인사해요	인사하세요	Please greet.
읽다	읽어요	읽으세요	Please read.

5. The honorific form of the copula 이다 'to be (equation)' is [N이세요] if the noun preceding it ends in a consonant and [N세요] if the noun ends in a vowel as in example (2).

Exercise

1. Give answers that are appropriate for the contexts. Use ~어요/아요 or ~(으)세요.

    (1)   The following questions are addressed to you. Answer the questions.

        대학생이세요?   _____

        한국어 숙제하세요?   _____

        친구가 많으세요?   _____

    (2)   Talking about Professor Lee.

        마이클: 이 선생님은 한국 사람이세요?

        리사: 네, _____

    (3)   제니: 선생님, 뭐 _____?

        선생님: 책 읽어요.

        제니: 오늘 수업 _____?

        선생님: 아니요, 없어요.

CULTURE

Korean national symbols

1. 태극기 (Korean national flag)

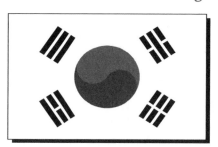

The 태극기 was first flown on August 22, 1882, by a Korean emissary to Japan, Pak Young-hyo. Since then, the shape of the flag has changed many times. It was officially declared the national flag of the Republic of Korea on October 15, 1949. The flag has a white background with a 태극 'the Great Absolute', the two-lobed yin-yang (in Korean, 음양) symbol, in the center, flanked by four of the Eight Trigrams from the *Book of Changes*. The 태극 symbolizes the philosophy of the dualism of the universe — the balance and harmony in nature of opposite forces and elements which are in perpetual motion. It represents the ultimate source of all existence and the basis of all values. The upper red lobe stands for yang (in Korean 양): positive, masculine, active, constructive, light, heat, and dignity, whereas the lower blue lobe stands for yin (in Korean 음): negative, feminine, passive, destructive, dark, cold, and hope. As for the black trigrams in each corner, the three solid bars of the upper left corner represent heaven, spring, east, and benevolence; the upper right bars, moon, winter, north, and wisdom; the lower right bars, earth, summer, west, and righteousness; and the lower left bars, sun, autumn, south, and etiquette. The flag as a whole symbolizes the ideal of the Korean people developing forever in harmony with the universe.

2. 무궁화 (Korean national flower)
The national flower of Korea is "the rose of Sharon." It is called 무궁화, which means the flower that never withers.

3. 애국가 (Korean national anthem)
The national anthem of Korea is 애국가. The Korean government in China, while Korea was under the Japanese rule, used the melody of the Scottish folk song "Auld Lang Syne." In 1948, the new song, written by 안익태, was chosen as the official national anthem.

Conversation 2 한국어를 공부해요.

소피아: 리사 씨, 안녕하세요?

          요즘 어떻게 지내세요?

리사: 잘 지내요. 소피아 씨는 어떻게 지내세요?

소피아: 저도 잘 지내요.

리사: 지금 뭐 하세요?

소피아: 오늘 한국어 시험이 있어요.

          그래서 한국어를^{G3.3} 공부해요.

리사: 아, 그래요?

          그럼, 열심히 공부하세요.

          그리고 시험^{G3.4} 잘 보세요.

소피아: 네.

NEW WORDS

NOUN		ADVERB	
공부(하다)	study	매일	every day
남자	man	어떻게	how
시험	test, exam	열심히	diligently
역사	history	요즘	these days
주스	juice	잘	well
텔레비전	television	지금	now
VERB		**PARTICLE**	
마시다	to drink	들	plural particle
만나다	to meet	을/를	object particle
보다(보세요)	to see, look, watch	**ADJECTIVE**	
지내다(지내세요)	to get along	맛없다	to be tasteless, not delicious
CONJUNCTION			
그래서	so, therefore	재미없다	to be uninteresting
그럼	(if so) then		

NEW EXPRESSIONS

1. 지내다 literally means 'to pass one's time'. 어떻게 지내세요? is an expression asking about the other party's well-being. It is comparable to 'How are you doing/getting along?' in English. In response, the other party may say 잘 지내요, meaning 'I'm doing fine'.

2. Verbs that end in 하다 'to do' such as 숙제하다 'to do homework' and 공부하다 'to study' are made of two elements: a noun and 하다 [N+하다]. These verbs are often used as a sequence of a noun + object particle 을/를 followed by 하다 [N을/를+하다], as in 숙제를 하다 and 공부를 하다.

3. When the verb 보다 'to see, look' is used with the noun 시험 'test, exam' as in 시험을 보다, it is interpreted as 'to take a test'.

4. Plural particle 들 is attached to nouns, as in 학생들, 선생님들, and 친구들. In Korean, the plurality is not mandatorily marked.

5. 그래서 'so, therefore' indicates a cause-effect relation between two sentences.

> 오늘은 수업이 없어요. 그래서 친구를 만나요.
> 내일 시험이 있어요. 그래서 공부해요.

Exercises

1. Fill in the blanks with appropriate question words 뭐, 누구, 어디, or 어떻게.

(1) A: 이름이 _____예요?
   B: 김유미예요.

(2) A: 사전이 _____ 있어요?
   B: 가방 안에 있어요.

(3) A: 요즘 _____ 지내세요?
   B: 잘 지내요.

(4) A: 한국어 선생님이 _____세요?
   B: 이민수 선생님이세요.

2. Complete the following sentences.

(1) 경제학 수업이 재미있어요. 그래서 _____

(2) 내일 역사 시험이 있어요. 그래서 _____

(3) 한국어 수업이 매일 있어요. 그래서 _____

(4) 학교 식당 커피가 맛있어요. 그래서 _____

GRAMMAR

G3.3 | The object particle 을/를

Examples

(1) 리사가 아침**을** 먹어요.

(2) 유미가 텔레비전**을** 봐요.

(3) 소피아가 매일 커피**를** 마셔요.

(4) 스티브가 친구**를** 만나요.

Notes

1. The particle 을/를 marks the object of the verb.

2. 을 is used when the object noun ends with a consonant and 를 with a vowel.

　　텔레비전**을** 봐요.
　　주스**를** 마셔요.

3. The basic sentence patterns: [N이/가　N을/를　V~어요/아요].

Subject (N이/가)	Object (N을/를)	Verb (V~어요/아요)
폴('Paul')**이**	아침**을**	먹어요.
마이클**이**	시험**을**	봐요.
리사**가**	커피**를**	마셔요.
유미**가**	친구**를**	만나요.

In the above examples, the subjects designate the actors, the ones who do the action, and the objects designate the things that the actors do something to.

Exercise

1. Fill in the blanks with appropriate particles 이/가 and 을/를.

　　(1)　　스티브가 매일 경제학을 공부해요.
　　(2)　　수잔_____ 교과서_____ 읽어요.
　　(3)　　제시카_____ 주스_____ 마셔요.
　　(4)　　제니_____ 남자 친구_____ 만나요.
　　(5)　　폴_____ 아침_____ 먹어요.
　　(6)　　미치코_____ 역사 숙제_____ 해요.

G3.4　Omission of particles

Examples

(1)　[statement]　　　　마이클은 여자 친구가 없어요.

　　　[conversation]　　유미:　　마이클 씨, 여자 친구 있어요?
　　　　　　　　　　　　마이클:　아니요, 없어요.

(2) [statement] 소피아는 일본 사람이 아니에요.

  [conversation] 유미: 소피아 씨, 일본 사람이에요?
  소피아: 아니요, 저 일본 사람 아니에요.

(3) [statement] 리사는 오늘 친구들을 만나요.

  [conversation] 스티브: 리사 씨, 오늘 뭐 하세요?
  리사: 친구들 만나요.

Notes

1. We have learned that nominals (nouns, pronouns, numerals, etc.) may be marked with a particle, such as 이/가 for subjects (G2.1) and 을/를 for objects (G3.3). In conversation, however, particles are frequently omitted.

2. When the purpose is to report "who does what to whom and when and where" in precise terms, the particle is usually needed.

3. In conversation, a particle is necessary when the speaker wants to focus on a specific element the speaker assumes the listener is not thinking of.

  소피아: 누가 책을 읽어요?
  마이클: 유미**가** 읽어요.

Exercises

1. Based on the given statement, complete the dialogues.

  (1) [Statement: 소피아는 역사를 공부해요. 그런데 재미없어요.]
  유미: 소피아 씨, 뭐 공부하세요?
  소피아: <u>역사 공부해요. 그런데 재미없어요.</u>

  (2) [Statement: 리사가 커피를 마셔요. 커피가 맛없어요.]
  스티브: 리사 씨, 뭐 하세요?
  리사: _____
  스티브: _____?
  리사: 아니요, 맛없어요.

(3)   [Statement: 유미는 지금 사전이 없어요. 집에 있어요.]

      스티브: 유미 씨, _____?

      유미: 아니요, 지금 없어요. 집에 있어요.

2. Write reporting statements based on the dialogues given.

(1)   스티브: 리사 씨, 뭐 하세요?

      리사: 아침 먹어요.

      [Statement: <u>리사**는** 아침**을** 먹어요.</u>]

(2)   리사: 제니 씨, 오늘 뭐 하세요?

      제니: 남자 친구 만나요. 리사 씨는 뭐 하세요?

      리사: 저는 텔레비전 봐요.

      [Statement: _____]

(3)   마이클: 소피아 씨, 한국어 교과서 있어요?

      소피아: 네, 있어요.

      마이클: 사전도 있어요?

      소피아: 네, 사전도 있어요.

      [Statement: _____]

Narration | 한국어 반

오늘 한국어 수업이 있어요. 교실이 유니온 빌딩 1층에
있어요. 유니온 빌딩은 도서관 앞에 있어요. 한국어 선생님은
이민수 선생님이세요. 선생님이 아주 좋으세요. 수업도 아주
재미있어요. 그런데 숙제가 많아요. 그래서 매일 한국어를
공부해요. 한국어 반에 학생들이 많아요. 중국 학생, 일본
학생이 많아요.

Exercises

1. Answer the following questions in Korean.

    (1)   한국어 교실이 어디 있어요?

    (2)   한국어 선생님이 누구세요?

    (3)   한국어 선생님이 어때요?

(4)   유니온 빌딩이 어디 있어요?

(5)   한국어 수업이 어때요?

(6)   한국어 반에 미국 학생이 많아요?

2. Fill in the blanks with the appropriate words provided below.

이/가	은/는	을/를	도	에
그래서	그리고	그런데		

오늘 한국어 수업_____ 있어요. 교실이 유니온 빌딩 1층_____ 있어요. 유니온 빌딩 _____ 도서관 앞에 있어요. 한국어 선생님_____ 이민수 선생님이세요. 선생님_____ 아주 좋으세요. 수업_____ 아주 재미있어요. _____ 숙제가 많아요. _____ 매일 한국어_____ 공부해요. 한국어 반_____ 학생들이 많아요. 중국 학생, 일본 학생_____ 많아요.

USAGE

A. Inquiring about someone's well-being

리사: 스티브 씨, 안녕하세요?
             요즘 어떻게 지내세요?
스티브: 잘 지내요. 리사 씨는 어때요?
리사: 저는 바빠요. (바쁘다 'to be busy')

Possible responses:

바빠요.	I'm busy.
그저 그래요.	Just so-so.
괜찮아요.	I'm all right / Not too bad.
좋아요.	I'm fine.
잘 지내요.	I'm doing well.

[Exercise] Pair off and exchange greetings, using some of the expressions above.

B. Talking about someone's major

There are three ways to ask and respond about someone's major:

1.   Generally asking what he/she studies:

     A: 뭐 공부해요/공부하세요?   What do you study?

     B: _____공부해요.

2.   Specifically asking what he/she majors in:

     A: 뭐 전공해요/전공하세요?   What do you major in?

     B: _____ 전공해요.

3.   Using an equational expression:

     A: 전공이 뭐예요?   What is your major?

     B: _____이에요/예요.

Some majors:

Humanities	Social sciences	Natural sciences	Engineering	Arts	Professional schools
동양학 Asian Studies	경제학 Economics	물리학 Physics	기계 공학 Mech. Engr.	음악 Music	건축학 Architecture
언어학 Linguistics	교육학 Education	생물학 Biology	전기 공학 Elect. Engr.	피아노 Piano	법학 Law

C. Describing people

Example   소피아 왕은 지금 2학년이에요. 중국 사람이에요.
              소피아 왕은 경제학을 공부해요. 한국어 반 학생이에요.
              그리고 집이 홍콩이에요.

[Exercise 1] Describe each of the people below based on the information given.

Name	Year	Nationality	Major	Status/ relationship	Hometown
소피아 왕	2학년	중국 사람	경제학	한국어 반 학생	홍콩 'Hong Kong'
스티브 윌슨	3학년	미국 사람	음악	한국어 반 학생	보스톤 'Boston'
마이클 정	1학년	한국 사람	컴퓨터	한국어 반 학생	뉴욕 'New York'
미치코 카노	4학년	일본 사람	동양학	스티브 친구	도쿄 'Tokyo'
제시카 김	1학년	한국 사람	생물학	소피아 친구	시카고 'Chicago'

[Exercise 2] First interview your classmates and fill in the chart below, then report the information to the class as in the example given above.

Name	Year	Nationality	Major	Status/ relationship	Hometown

D. Making requests

In a polite request you need to use the ~(으)세요 ending to show respect for the listener. Study some of the instructions or requests used in the classroom.

책을 펴세요.

책을 덮으세요.

칠판을 보세요.
칠판 'blackboard'

따라하세요.

잘 들으세요.

읽으세요.

쓰세요.

Requests that can be used by students:

다시 한 번 말씀해 주세요.	Please say that again.
크게 말씀해 주세요.	Please speak louder.
천천히 말씀해 주세요.	Please speak slowly.

[Exercise 1] Follow the instructions.

(1)　　책을 읽으세요.

(2)　　따라하세요.

(3)　　책을 펴세요.

(4)　　칠판에 쓰세요.

[Exercise 2] Make a request/instruction appropriate to the situation.

    (1)   You cannot hear the teacher's voice clearly.

    _____

    (2)   You did not hear what the teacher said.

    _____

    (3)   Please, repeat after me.

    _____

    (4)   You cannot follow the teacher's explanation because it is too fast.

    _____

    (5)   Please, close your book.

    _____

    (6)   Please, listen carefully.

    _____

Lesson 3 Korean Language Class

CONVERSATION 1: Do you have class today?

Jenny: Michael, do you have class today?
Michael: Yes, I have Korean class today. How about you, Jenny?
Jenny: I don't have any class today, but I have economics class tomorrow. Is your Korean class interesting?
Michael: Yes, it's very interesting and the teacher is nice.
Jenny: Who is the teacher?
Michael: Professor Minsoo Lee.
Jenny: Are there many students in the class?
Michael: Yes, there are.

CONVERSATION 2: I'm studying Korean.

Sophia: Hi, Lisa. How are you these days?
Lisa: I'm doing well. How are you these days, Sophia?
Sophia: I'm also doing well.
Lisa: What are you doing now?
Sophia: I have a Korean exam today. So I'm studying Korean.
Lisa: Oh, really? Then study hard. And good luck on your exam.
Sophia: Okay.

NARRATION: Korean class

I have Korean class today. The classroom is located on the first floor of the Union Building. The Union Building is in front of the library. My Korean teacher is Professor Minsoo Lee. He is very nice. The class is also very interesting, but there is a lot of homework. So I study Korean every day. There are many students in the Korean class. There are several Chinese and Japanese students.

4과 집 [At Home]

| Conversation 1 | 동생이 두 명 있어요. |

소피아: 스티브 씨, 집이 어디예요?

스티브: 보스톤이에요.

아버지하고 어머니가 보스톤에 계세요.

소피아 씨 부모님은 어디 계세요?

소피아: 홍콩에 계세요.

오빠하고 동생도 홍콩에 있어요.

오빠는 대학원생이에요.

그리고 동생은 지금 고등학생이에요.

스티브: 남동생이에요, 여동생이에요?G4.1

소피아: 여동생이에요. 스티브 씨도 동생 있어요?

스티브: 네, 여동생 한G4.2 명하고 남동생 두 명G4.3 이

있어요.

NEW WORDS

NOUN		COUNTER	
개	① dog	개	② item
고등학생	high school student	권	volume
남동생	younger brother	년	year
대학원생	graduate student	달	month
동생	younger sibling	달러	dollar (=불)
보스톤	Boston	마리	animal
부모님	parents	명	people
아버지	father	원 (₩)	won (Korean currency)
어머니	mother	월	month
여동생	younger sister	일	② day
오빠	the older brother of a female	**NUMBER**	
형	the older brother of a male	두 (with counter)	two (=둘)
홍콩	Hong Kong	한 (with counter)	one (=하나)
		VERB	
PRE-NOUN		계시다 *hon.* (계세요)	to be (existence), stay
몇	how many, what	**PARTICLE**	
	(with a counter)	하고	① and (with nouns)

NEW EXPRESSIONS

1. 계시다 is the honorific word for 있다 'to be (existence)'. It is used when the subject is a respected person, e.g., a teacher, a parent, a grandparent, and so on.

2. The honorific forms of 있어요/ 없어요 for the meaning of possession are 있으세요/ 없으세요 while those for the meaning of existence are 계세요/ 안 계세요. Remember that the honorific form of the copula 이다 'to be' is 이세요/ 세요.

[identification]
리사는 학생이에요.   vs.   이민수 선생님은 한국어 선생님이세요.

[existence]
리사는 집에 있어요.   vs.   이민수 선생님은 집에 계세요.

[possession]
리사는 동생이 있어요.   vs.   이민수 선생님은 동생이 있으세요.

3. In Korean, proper references for siblings depend on the sex of both the sibling and the self, as well as their relative ages. 동생 'younger sibling', however, can be used to refer to either a male (남동생) or a female (여동생).

For a male   For a female

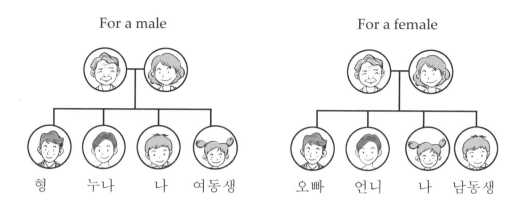

형   누나   나   여동생   오빠   언니   나   남동생

4. 하고 'and' joins nouns.

5. The terms 학교 and 학생 refer to 'school' and student' respectively. These terms are used with suffixes to indicate different educational levels such as 초등학교/초등학생 'elementary school (student)', 중학교/중학생 'middle school (student)', 고등학교/고등학생 'high school (student)', and 대학교/대학생 'college (student)'. The only exception is 대학원/대학원생 'graduate school (student)'.

Exercises

1. Fill in the blanks with native Korean numbers and proper counters.

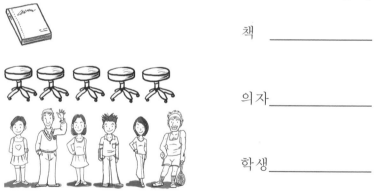

책   _____

의자_____

학생_____

2. Who's who in the family? Describe each family member from Sally's perspective.

샐리

GRAMMAR

G4.1 | Alternative questions

Examples

(1) 스티브: 소피아는 **일본 사람이에요, 중국 사람이에요?**
   유미: 중국 사람이에요.

(2) 마이클: 동생이 **있어요, 없어요?**
   소피아: 남동생이 있어요.

Alternative questions are used to ask someone to choose one from the given choices.

Exercise

1. Create alternative questions.

(1) 마이클: 소피아 씨는 <u>1학년이에요, 2학년이에요?</u>
   소피아: 2학년이에요.

(2) 마이클: 소피아 씨는＿＿＿＿＿＿＿＿＿＿＿＿＿＿＿
   소피아: 중국 사람이에요.

(3) 소피아: 형이＿＿＿＿＿＿＿＿＿＿＿＿＿＿＿＿＿
   스티브: 두 명이에요.

(4) 리사: 부모님은＿＿＿＿＿＿＿＿＿＿＿＿＿＿＿
   소피아: 홍콩에 계세요.

(5) 유미: 집이 ＿＿＿＿＿＿＿＿＿＿＿＿＿＿＿＿＿
   리사: 보스톤이에요.

(6) 소피아: 스티브 씨는＿＿＿＿＿＿＿＿＿＿＿＿＿＿
   스티브: 역사 공부해요.

| G4.2 | Numbers |

Korean uses two sets of numbers: Sino-Korean numbers and native Korean numbers.

Arabic numeral	Sino-Korean	Native Korean	Native Korean before counters
1	일	하나	한
2	이	둘	두
3	삼	셋	세
4	사	넷	네
5	오	다섯	다섯
6	육	여섯	여섯
7	칠	일곱	일곱
8	팔	여덟 [여덜]	여덟
9	구	아홉	아홉
10	십	열	열
11	십일	열하나	열한
12	십이	열둘	열두
13	십삼	열셋	열세
14	십사	열넷	열네
15	십오	열다섯	열다섯
16	십육 [심뉵]	열여섯	열여섯
17	십칠	열일곱	열일곱
18	십팔	열여덟	열여덟
19	십구	열아홉	열아홉
20	이십	스물	스무
30	삼십	서른	서른
40	사십	마흔	마흔
50	오십	쉰	쉰
60	육십	예순	예순
70	칠십	일흔	일흔
80	팔십	여든	여든
90	구십	아흔	아흔
100	백		
1,000	천		
10,000	만		

1. Some native Korean numbers have two forms, depending on whether they are followed by a counter or used in isolation.

하나 → 한 (명)   둘 → 두 (명)   셋 → 세 (명)
넷 → 네 (명)   스물→ 스무 (명)

2. For multiples of 100, 1,000, 10,000, and more, only Sino-Korean numbers are used.

100	백	200	이백
1,000	천	2,000	이천
10,000	만	20,000	이만
100,000	십만	200,000	이십만
1,000,000	백만	2,000,000	이백만
10,000,000	천만	20,000,000	이천만
100,000,000	억	200,000,000	이억

일 달러는 천 원이에요.   One dollar is (equivalent to) 1,000 won.
텔레비전이 백구십만 원이에요.   The television costs 1,900,000 won.
한국 인구는 오천만이에요.   The population of Korea is 50 million.
서울 인구는 천사십만이에요.   The population of Seoul is 10.4 million.

G4.3   Noun counters

Examples

(1)   제니: 한국어 교실이 몇 **층**에 있어요?
       리사: **2층**에 있어요.
       제니: 학생이 많아요?
       리사: 스무 **명**이에요.

(2)   교실에 의자가 여덟 **개** 있어요.

(3)   제니는 책이 다섯 **권** 있어요.

(4)   저는 형이 한 **명** 있어요.

(5)   내일 시험이 **하나** 있어요.

Notes

1. When you count, you must use different counters. Nouns are classified into

many groups depending on shape or kind. As indicated in G4.2, the following five native Korean numbers have slightly different forms when used with counters: 하나 → 한, 둘 → 두, 셋 → 세, 넷 → 네, 스물 → 스무. There is no change in 스물 as in 스물한 명, 스물두 명, and so on.

Some counters take Sino-Korean numbers, and others take native numbers. For example, 5층 is read as 오 층 (with a Sino-Korean number) while 5명 is read as 다섯 명 (with a native Korean number).

Some counters can be used either with Sino or native Korean numbers in higher numbers; for example, 20명 may be read as 이십 명 as well as 스무 명. The following tables show the counters used with the two different types of numbers.

Counters used with native Korean numbers:

Counter	Kinds of things counted	Counting
명/사람	people	한 명, 두 명, 세 명 . . .
마리	animals	한 마리, 두 마리, 세 마리 . . .
개	items	한 개, 두 개, 세 개 . . .
권	volumes	한 권, 두 권, 세 권 . . .
과	lessons (for counting)	한 과, 두 과, 세 과 (three lessons) . . .
시간	hours (for duration)	한 시간, 두 시간, 세 시간 . . .
달	months	한 달, 두 달, 세 달 (three months) . . .

Counters used with Sino-Korean numbers:

Counter	Kinds of things counted	Counting
층	floors, layers	일 층, 이 층, 삼 층 . . .
과	lesson number	일 과, 이 과, 삼 과 (lesson 3) . . .
원	won (Korean currency)	십 원, 백 원, 천 원, 만 원 . . .
학년	school year, grade	일학년, 이학년, 삼학년 . . .
년	year	일 년, 이 년, 삼 년 . . .
월	month (for date)	일월(January), 이월(February) . . .
일	day (for date)	일일 (the 1st as in 삼월 일일), 이일, 삼일 . . .

2. 몇 is the question word for quantity, and almost always is followed by a counter: 몇 층, 몇 명, 몇 마리, 몇 권, 몇 시간, and so on.

For 원 and 달러/불, 얼마 'how much' is used instead of 몇 원 and 몇 달러/불.

3. Word order in counting is [noun + particle + number + counter].

Noun	Particle	Number	Counter	Verb
오빠	가	두	명	
가방	이	세	개	
책	이	네	권	있어요
개	가	한	마리	
책상	이	다섯	개	

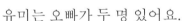

유미는 오빠가 두 명 있어요.

가방이 세 개 있어요.

4. 삼 과 refers to 'lesson 3' as in 오늘 3과 공부해요 'I (will) study lesson 3 today' while 세 과 refers to 'three lessons' as in 오늘 세 과 공부해요 'I (will) study three lessons'.

Exercise

1. Answer each question in Korean, using the proper counter.

    (1)   How many books do you have at home?

             집에 (책이) 백 권 있어요.

    (2)   How many students are there in the Korean class?

    (3)   What lesson do we study today?

    (4)   How many lessons are there in the History textbook?

    (5)   On which floor is the Korean-language classroom?

    (6)   How many watches do you have?

    (7)   How many Korean friends do you have?

Conversation 2   누구 방이에요?

(Sophia visits Lisa's apartment.)

소피아: 리사 씨, 아파트에 방이 몇 개 있어요?

리사: 세 개 있어요.

소피아: 룸메이트 있어요?

리사: 네, 두 명 있어요.

소피아: 룸메이트도 학생이에요?

리사: 네, 제니하고 유미는 생물학을 공부해요.

그리고 제니는 제 한국어 반 친구예요.

룸메이트들하고 저는 사이가 아주 좋아요.

소피아: 이건 누구 방이에요?G4.4

리사: 제 방이에요.

소피아: 방이 참 예뻐요.G4.5

리사: 고마워요.

NEW WORDS

NOUN		ADJECTIVE	
거	thing (contraction of 것)	고맙다(고마워요)	to be thankful
누나	the older sister of a male	나쁘다	to be bad
뉴욕	New York	비싸다	to be expensive
룸메이트	roommate	예쁘다 (예뻐요)	to be pretty
방	room	작다	to be small (in size)
사이	① relationship;	**VERB**	
	② between	배우다	to learn
생물학	biology	오다	to come
아파트	apartment	자다	to sleep
언니	the older sister of a female	주다	to give
로스앤젤레스	Los Angeles (L.A.)	**PRONOUN**	
하와이	Hawai'i	저희 *hum.*	we/us/our (=우리 *plain*)
PARTICLE		이거	this (= 이것)
만	only	제 *hum.*	my (=내 *plain*)
의	of		

NEW EXPRESSIONS

1. 거 is the contracted form of 것 (lit. 'thing'). In general, 거 is used in colloquial speech, and 것 is used in writing and in formal situations. 이건 is also the contracted form of [이거 'this thing' +는 (topic particle)].

2. The dictionary form of 고마워요 is 고맙다. Note that /ㅂ/ in 고맙다 becomes 우 when followed by ~어요.

Exercise

1. Choose as many nouns as possible that match the adjectives provided, and then write them in the corresponding boxes.

누나   룸메이트   방   사이   아파트   언니

나빠요	비싸요	예뻐요	작아요

GRAMMAR

G4.4	Expressing possessive relations: N1(possessor) N2 (possessed)

Examples

(1) 제니: 이거 **누구 사전**이에요?   Whose dictionary is this?
     유미: **스티브 거**예요.   It's Steve's.

(2) 선생님: 이거 **마이클 책**이에요?   Michael, is this your book?
     마이클: 네, **제 거**예요.   Yes, it's mine.

(3) 리사: 소피아 씨, 가방이 참 예뻐요.   Sophia, your bag is very pretty.

     소피아: **제 동생 거**예요.   It's my younger sibling's.

(4) 소피아: 언니만 뉴욕에 있어요?   Is only your older sister in New York?

     리사: 네, **저희 아버지, 어머니**는   Yes, my father and mother are
              로스앤젤레스에 계세요.   in Los Angeles.

Notes

1. Possession involves two parts, the possessor and the possessed. The most common way of expressing the possessive relation is to place the possessor and the possessed side by side.

possessor	possessed	
마이클	책	Michael's book
우리	아버지, 어머니	my (our) father and mother
학생	이름	the student's name

2. The possessive particle 의 (usually pronounced [에]), comparable to the English preposition 'of', may be used sometimes but usually not in conversation. However, it is used in limited contexts, mostly when both the possessor and the possessed refer to abstract concepts.

미국의 대통령	the president of the United States of America
영국의 수도	the capital of the U.K.
오늘의 뉴스	the news of the day

3. The possessive pronouns 내 and 제 are formed by combining the regular pronouns 나 and 저 with the particle 의. Sometimes contractions occur.

	I	my
Plain	나	내 (나 + 의)
Humble	저	제 (저 + 의)

The possessive particle 의 is often omitted in 누구의 'whose', as in 누구 시계예요?

4. When the possessed object is obvious from the preceding context, 거/것, which literally means 'thing', can substitute for it.

A:	이거 누구 책이에요?	Whose book is this?
B:	스티브 책이에요.	(It's) Steve's book.
	스티브 거예요.	(It's) Steve's.

When 거 is combined with possessive pronouns, it creates the equivalent of English mine and ours.

내	my (plain)	+ 거	=	내 거	mine (lit. my thing)
제	my (humble)	+ 거	=	제 거	mine (lit. my thing)
우리	our (plain)	+ 거	=	우리 거	ours (lit. our thing)
저희	our (humble)	+ 거	=	저희 거	ours (lit. our thing)

Note that for the equivalent of English yours, his, and hers, the person's name is used instead of the pronouns:

마이클:	이거 스티브 씨 우산이에요?	Is this your umbrella, Steve?
스티브:	네, 제 거예요.	Yes, it's mine.
마이클:	이거 스티브 책이에요?	Is this Steve's book?
리사:	네, 스티브 거예요.	Yes, it's Steve's.

Exercises

1. Using the given subject and item, formulate sentences in both the plain form and the humble form when necessary.

(1)	나 / 방	내 방이에요./제 방이에요.
(2)	유미 / 언니	_____
(3)	리사 / 사전	_____
(4)	우리 / 형	_____
(5)	나 / 친구	_____

2. Complete the dialogue using 거.

<blockquote>

(1)   A: 누구 가방이에요?

       B: [마이클] <u>마이클 거예요.</u>

(2)   A: 이거 누구 책이에요?

       B: [스티브] _____

(3)   A: 이거 누구 사전이에요?

       B: [나] _____

(4)   A: [컴퓨터] _____?

       B: 제 동생 거예요.

</blockquote>

| G4.5 | Vowel contraction |

Examples

(1)   A: 오늘 뭐 **해요**?
       B: 친구를 **만나요**.

(2)   A: 요즘 어떻게 **지내세요**?
       B: 잘 **지내요**.

(3)   유미: 지금 뭐 **하세요**?
       마이클: 커피 **마셔요**.

(4)   제니: 스티브 씨는 뭐 **배우세요**?
       스티브: 생물학 **배워요**.

(5)   마이클: 제니 씨, 대학교 캠퍼스가 **커요**?
       제니: 아니요, **작아요**.

Notes

When two vowels meet in verb/adjective conjugation, vowel contraction frequently occurs.

1. Two identical vowels (아 + 아) become a single vowel.

<blockquote>

가   +   ~~아~~요   →   가요

자   +   ~~아~~요   →   자요

</blockquote>

만나   +   어요   →   만나요
싸   +   어요   →   싸요
비싸   +   어요   →   비싸요

2. 애 causes the following 어 to be dropped.

지내   +   어요   →   지내요

3. The sequence 이 + 어 is contracted to 여.

마시   +   어요   →   마셔요

The honorific 시 + 어, however, is contracted to 세 instead of 셔.

안녕하시 + 어요   →   안녕하세요
계시   +   어요   →   계세요

4. The following combinations may be contracted to diphthongs.

우   +   어   →   워
오   +   아   →   와

The contraction is *optional* when the preceding syllable begins with a consonant.

주   +   어요   →   줘요 (주어요 is also allowed.)
보   +   아요   →   봐요 (보아요 is also allowed.)

The contraction is *obligatory* when there is no consonant.

오   +   아요   →   와요
배우   +   어요   →   배워요

5. Verbs and adjectives whose stems end in 으 lose the 으 before another vowel.

크다   +   어요   →   커요
나쁘다 +   아요   →   나빠요

Exercises

1. Add the polite ending ~어요/아요 to each predicate.

(1)   학교에('to') (가다)   학교에 가요.

(2)   주스를 (마시다).   _____

(3)   텔레비전을 (보다).   _____

(4)   부모님이 하와이에 (계시다).   _____

(5)   오늘 남자 친구를 (만나다).   _____

(6)   내일 형이 (오다).   _____

(7)   언니하고 중국어를 (배우다).   _____

(8)   책하고 사전을 (주다).   _____

(9)   누나가 지금 (자다).   _____

(10)   컴퓨터가 아주 (비싸다).   _____

2. Give the polite ending for each 으 adjective.

(1)   방이 (크다)   _____

(2)   시계가 (예쁘다)   _____

(3)   아파트가 (나쁘다)   _____

CULTURE

1. Korean collectivism: 우리 집, 우리 나라, 우리 반, 우리 학교
Certain objects, people, or concepts do not necessarily belong to one individual, but to a group of people, such as a nation, school, family, house, classes, etc. In Korean, the possessor of these items frequently reflects this 'group possession' in speech, referring to them with a plural possessive pronoun 우리 (or its humble form 저희) 'we/us/our', opposed to the singular 나 (or its humble form 저) 'I/my/mine'. This is frequently the case even when the speaker may be speaking of only one person or him/herself, as in 우리 아내 'my wife'. Compare English and Korean.

English	Korean
my/our country	우리 나라
my/our house	우리 집
my/our family	우리 가족
my/our father/mother	우리 아버지/어머니
my/our class	우리 반
my/our school	우리 학교

2. The Traditional Korean House: 한옥과 온돌

The traditional Korean house is called 한옥. Koreans used thatch or tiles for the roof, and earth or timber for the walls. 온돌 is a traditional floor-heating system in Korea. To make a traditional 온돌 room, flat stones are placed on the floor of the room. Then earth is put on the stones and made flat. Heat from the cookstove heats the stone. Once it is heated, it keeps warm for quite a long time. It is a very hygienic and effective way of heating rooms. However, you can see the traditional 온돌 house only in the remote rural areas in modern Korea because most Koreans live in high-rise apartments.

아궁이 'fire hole'

온돌 'under floor heating'

Narration | 내 친구 소피아

소피아는 우리 반 친구예요. 한국어하고 경제학을 공부해요. 소피아는 중국 사람이에요. 집이 홍콩이에요. 홍콩에 아버지하고 어머니가 계세요. 그리고 오빠하고 동생도 홍콩에 있어요. 소피아만 미국에 있어요. 소피아 오빠는 대학원생이에요. 생물학을 공부해요. 소피아 여동생은 고등학생이에요. 소피아하고 소피아 동생은 사이가 참 좋아요.

Exercises

1. Read the narration and answer the following questions.
   - (1)   소피아는 무엇을 공부해요?
   - (2)   소피아는 지금 어디 있어요?
   - (3)   홍콩에 누가 있어요?
   - (4)   소피아 오빠는 무엇을 공부해요?
   - (5)   소피아 동생은 소피아하고 사이가 어때요?

2. Draw Sophia's family tree based on the narration.

3. Fill in the blanks with the appropriate particles provided below.

| 이/가 | 은/는 | 도 | 에 | 을/를 | 만 | 하고 |

소피아_____ 우리 반 친구예요. 한국어_____ 경제학_____ 공부해요.

소피아_____ 중국 사람이에요. 집_____ 홍콩이에요. 홍콩_____ 아버지_____

어머니_____ 계세요. 그리고 오빠_____ 동생_____ 홍콩_____ 있어요.

소피아_____ 미국_____ 있어요. 소피아 오빠_____ 대학원생이에요.

생물학_____ 공부해요. 소피아 여동생_____ 고등학생이에요. 소피아_____

소피아 동생_____ 사이_____ 참 좋아요.

USAGE

A. Inquiring about hometown and family

스티브:	소피아 씨는 집이 어디예요?
소피아:	홍콩이에요.
스티브:	홍콩에 부모님이 계세요?
소피아:	네. 부모님은 홍콩에 계세요.
	스티브 씨는 집이 어디예요?
스티브:	우리 집은 보스톤이에요.
	보스톤에 아버지, 어머니하고, 누나, 형이 있어요.
소피아:	동생은 없어요?
스티브:	없어요.

(1)　　　Asking about and describing someone's hometown:

　　　　A:　　　[person]은/는 집이 어디예요?
　　　　B:　　　우리 집은 [place]이에요/예요.

(2)　　　Asking about family members:

　　　　A:　　　_____있어요?
　　　　B:　　　네, 있어요 / 아니요, 없어요.

(3)　　　Describing where family members live, using the honorific verb 계세요
　　　　for parents:

A: 부모님은 어디 계세요?
B: _____에 계세요.

A: _____은/는 어디 있어요?
B: _____에 있어요.

A: _____에 누가 있어요?
B: _____이/가 있어요 / _____이/가 계세요.

[Exercise] Ask your partner about his or her hometown and family.

B. Asking and telling about quantity/counting

If one wants to ask for an unspecified number, the question word 몇 is used.

    (1)   A: 한국어 교실이 몇 층이에요?
               B: 2층이에요.

    (2)   A: 몇 학년이에요?
               B: 1학년이에요.

[Exercise 1] Ask your partner the following questions.

    (1)   한국어 반 학생이 몇 명이에요?
    (2)   오늘은 몇 과 공부해요?
    (3)   집에 책이 몇 권 있어요?
    (4)   몇 학년이에요?
    (5)   친구가 몇 명 있어요?

[Exercise 2] Count the given items aloud.

    (1)   school years from 1st to 12th grade
    (2)   number of students in class
    (3)   number of floors in the building
    (4)   number of desks in the classroom
    (5)   number of lessons in your Korean textbook

[Exercise 3] Make up a question that is appropriate for each response.

(1)   A: <u>한국 학생이 몇 명이에요?</u>
      B: 20명이에요.

(2)   A: _____?
      B: 3층에 있어요.

(3)   A: _____?
      B: 15명이에요.

(4)   A: _____?
      B: 4과를 공부해요.

(5)   A: _____?
      B: 2학년이에요.

[Exercise 4] Practice the following dialogue using the appropriate numeral expressions.

A: _____은/는 얼마예요?   How much is ____?
B: _____불 ____센트예요.   It's ____ dollars and ____ cents.

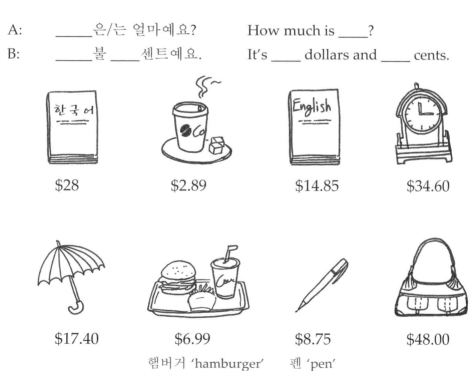

$28 $2.89 $14.85 $34.60

$17.40 $6.99 $8.75 $48.00

          햄버거 'hamburger'   펜 'pen'

Lesson 4 At Home

CONVERSATION 1: I have two younger siblings

Sophia:	Steve, where is your home?
Steve:	It's in Boston. My parents are in Boston. Sophia, where are your parents?
Sophia:	They are in Hong Kong. My siblings are also in Hong Kong. My older brother is a graduate student, and my younger sibling is a high school student.
Steve:	Is that a brother or sister?
Sophia:	It's a younger sister. Do you have any younger siblings?
Steve:	Yes, I have one younger sister and two younger brothers.

CONVERSATION 2: Whose room is it?
(Sophia visits Lisa's apartment.)

Sophia:	Lisa, how many rooms are there in your apartment?
Lisa:	There are three rooms.
Sophia:	Do you have any roommates?
Lisa:	Yes, I have two roommates.
Sophia:	Are your roommates also students?
Lisa:	Yes, Jenny and Yumi study biology, and Jenny is my classmate in Korean class. My roommates and I are very close.
Sophia:	Whose room is this?
Lisa:	It's my room.
Sophia:	Your room is very lovely.
Lisa:	Thank you.

NARRATION: My friend Sophia

Sophia is my classmate. She studies Korean and biology. Sophia is Chinese. Her home is in Hong Kong. Her father and mother live in Hong Kong. Her older brother and younger sister are also in Hong Kong. Sophia is the only one in the United States. Sophia's older brother is a graduate student studying biology. Her younger sister is a high school student. Sophia and her younger sister are very close.

5과 서점에서   [At the Bookstore]

| Conversation 1 | 서점에서 친구를 만나요. |

제니: 리사 씨, 안녕하세요?

리사: 어, 제니 씨, 오래간만이에요.

제니: 네, 오래간만이에요.

         그런데 어디 가세요?

리사: 커피숍에^{G5.1} 가요.

         제니 씨는 어디 가세요?

제니: 저는 서점에 가요.

         친구가 학교 앞 서점에서^{G5.1} 일을 해요.^{G5.2}

리사: 아, 그래요? 그럼, 내일 학교에서 봐요.

제니: 네, 안녕히 가세요.

NEW WORDS

NOUN			
공원	park	테니스	tennis
랩	lab	햄버거	hamburger
백화점	department store	**VERB**	
생일	birthday	가르치다	to teach
서점	bookstore (=책방)	사다	to buy
선물(하다)	present, gift	치다	to play (tennis)
쇼핑(하다)	shopping	**PARTICLE**	
연습(하다)	practice	에	② to (destination)
오래간만	after a long time	에서	① in, at
운동(하다)	exercise		(dynamic location)
일(하다)	③ work	**ADVERB**	
저녁	① evening; ② dinner	안녕히	in peace
점심	lunch	**CONJUNCTION**	
커피숍	coffee shop, cafe	그런데	② by the way

NEW EXPRESSIONS

1. 오래간만이에요/오랜만이에요 is an expression used when two people meet after a long while. It is equivalent to 'It's been a long while', or more colloquially, 'Long time no see' in English.

2. 안녕히 가세요, literally meaning 'go in peace', is a greeting used when two people leave each other from a neutral place. If the place belongs to one of the parties, the one staying in his/her territory says 안녕히 **가세요** 'go in peace', and the person leaving says 안녕히 **계세요** 'stay in peace'.

3. The locative particle 에 is often deleted when used together with the question word 어디, as shown in the following examples.

> 어디(에) 가세요?
> 어디(에)서 친구를 만나요?

4. 그런데 'but, however' is also used as 'by the way' when the speaker shifts from one topic to another.

> 유미: 제니 씨, 뭐 해요?
> 제니: 아침 먹어요.
>   **그런데**, 스티브는 어디 있어요?
> 유미: 도서관에 있어요.

Exercises

1. Fill in the blanks with appropriate words.

    (1)   리사는 _____에서 숙제를 해요

    (2)   유미는 _____에서 친구를 만나요.

    (3)   마이클은 _____에서 일을 해요.

    (4)   제니는 _____에서 아침을 먹어요.

2. Answer the following questions.

    (1)   어디서 점심을 먹어요?

    (2)   어디서 책을 읽어요?

    (3)   어디서 한국어 수업을 해요?

    (4)   어디서 커피를 마셔요?

GRAMMAR

G5.1 The locative particles 에 and 에서

Examples

[static location: 에]

(1) A: 형은 어디 있어요?
      B: 로스앤젤레스**에** 있어요.

(2) A: 부모님은 어디 계세요?
      B: 집**에** 계세요.

[destination/goal: 에]

(3) 리사: 유미 씨, 어디 가세요?
      유미: 우체국**에** 가요.
            리사 씨는 어디 가세요?
      리사: 컴퓨터 랩**에** 가요.

[dynamic location: 에서]

(4)   A: 어디에서 운동해요?
       B: 공원에서 운동해요.

(5)   A: 생일 선물을 어디에서 사요?
       B: 백화점에서 사요.

(6)   A: 어디서 테니스를 쳐요?
       B: 공원에서 쳐요.

Notes

1. Recall from G2.2 that the locative particle 에 is used to indicate where an entity exists, as in (1) and (2). In these cases, the particle 에 indicates a static location and the simple existence of an entity.

2. The particle 에 is also used to indicate destination or goal, typically for directional verbs such as 가다 'to go' and 오다 'to come' (e.g., [place]에 가요/와요) as in example (3).

3. A different particle 에서 is used to indicate the location of activity. It refers to a dynamic location, because the action or activity takes place in that location as in (4)–(6). Compare the usage of 에 and 에서 in the following examples.

도서관에 있어요.   [static location]
도서관에 가요.   [goal]
도서관에서 공부해요.   [dynamic location]

As shown here, the particle 에 is used with the existence verb 있다 and the directional verbs 오다/가다, while the particle 에서 is used with action verbs such as 공부하다, 운동하다, 먹다, and 일하다.

Exercises

1. Answer each question according to the images.

(1)   (2)   (3)   (4)   (5)

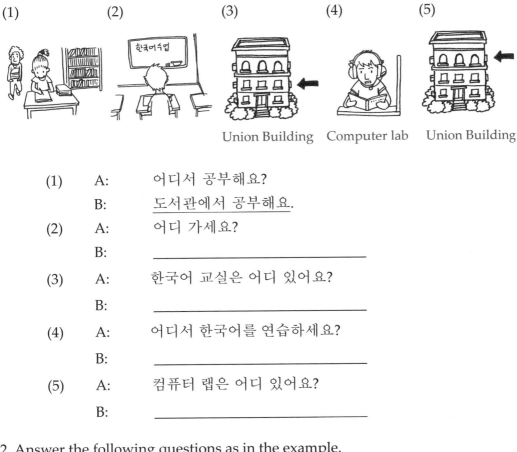

Union Building   Computer lab   Union Building

(1)   A: 어디서 공부해요?

       B: <u>도서관에서 공부해요.</u>

(2)   A: 어디 가세요?

       B: _____

(3)   A: 한국어 교실은 어디 있어요?

       B: _____

(4)   A: 어디서 한국어를 연습하세요?

       B: _____

(5)   A: 컴퓨터 랩은 어디 있어요?

       B: _____

2. Answer the following questions as in the example.

(1)   (2)   (3)   (4)

(1)   유미는 어디서 쇼핑해요?

       <u>백화점에서 쇼핑해요.</u>

(2)   폴은 어디서 점심 먹어요?

_____

(3)   제시카는 어디서 커피 마셔요?

_____

(4)   수지는 어디서 저녁을 먹어요?

_____

G5.2   The basic sentence pattern

Examples

(1)   리사**가** 식당**에서** 햄버거**를** 먹어요.

(2)   오빠**가** 방**에서** 텔레비전**을** 봐요.

(3)   이민수 선생님**이** 대학교**에서** 한국어**를** 가르치세요.

Note

1. The basic word order of Korean is different from that of English. Korean is a subject-object-verb language, whereas English is a subject-verb-object language. For example, the word order of the sentence 'Yumi studies Korean in the classroom' is as follows:

Who (subject)	Where (complement)	What (object)	To do (verb)
유미**가**	교실**에서**	한국어**를**	공부해요.
Yumi	in the classroom	Korean	study

The word order is flexible as long as the predicate is placed at the end.

유미**가**	교실**에서**	한국어**를**	공부해요.
유미**가**	한국어**를**	교실**에서**	공부해요.
교실**에서**	유미**가**	한국어**를**	공부해요.
교실**에서**	한국어**를**	유미**가**	공부해요.
한국어**를**	유미**가**	교실**에서**	공부해요.
한국어**를**	교실**에서**	유미**가**	공부해요.

Exercise

1. Look at the pictures and say what each person is doing where.

(1)   (2)   (3)   (4)   (5)

(1)   리사가 방에서 전화를 해요 ('to talk on the phone').

(2)   제니_____

(3)   유미_____

(4)   수지_____

(5)   스티브_____

Conversation 2   선물 사러 백화점에 가요.

소피아: 마이클 씨, 오늘 뭐 하세요?

마이클: 친구 생일 선물 사러 백화점에 가요.[G5.3]

소피아: 친구 생일이 언제예요?

마이클: 이번 토요일이에요.

　　　　　소피아 씨는 오늘 뭐 하세요?

소피아: 저는 오전에 수업 들으러[G5.4] 학교에 가요.

마이클: 수업이 몇 시에 있어요?

소피아: 10시에 있어요.

마이클: 그럼, 오후에 저하고 같이 백화점에 가요.

소피아: 네, 좋아요.

마이클: 3시 30분 괜찮아요?

소피아: 네, 괜찮아요.

NEW WORDS

NOUN		VERB	
가게	store	걷다	to walk
오전	a.m.	듣다 (들으러)	① to listen; ② to take a course
오후	afternoon	좋아하다	to like
옷	clothes	**COUNTER**	
월요일	Monday	과목	course, subject
화요일	Tuesday	분	minute
수요일	Wednesday	시	hour, o'clock
목요일	Thursday	**ADVERB**	
금요일	Friday	같이	together
토요일	Saturday	언제	when
일요일	Sunday	**PARTICLE**	
정치학	political science	에	③ at, in, on (time)
이번	this time	하고	② with
학기	semester, academic term	**SUFFIX**	
		~(으)러	in order to

NEW EXPRESSIONS

1. In [course/subject]을/를 들어요, 듣다/들어요 literally means 'to listen'.

  이번 학기에 한국어 수업을 들어요.
  I am taking Korean class this semester.

2. [N하고 같이] is parallel to 'together with N' in English.

3. 시 occurs with native Korean numbers, and 분 occurs with Sino-Korean numbers.

Native Korean numbers	Sino-Korean numbers
12시	**50분**
열두 시	오십 분

4. In English, the time of day is divided into a.m. and p.m. However, in Korean the time of day is stated in detail: 오전 10시 (10 a.m.); 오후 3시 (3 p.m.); 저녁 'evening' 7시 (7 p.m.); 밤 'night' 11시 (11 p.m.); and 새벽 'dawn' 4시 (4 a.m.).

5. Note that 30 분 can also be stated as 반 'half': 6시 30분 = 6시 반.

6. The particle 에 'at' is also used to specify a time reference. However, 어제 'yesterday', 오늘, and 내일 cannot occur with 에.

3시에 수업이 있어요.	I have a class at three o'clock.
오늘에 수업이 있어요.	I have a class today.

Exercises

1. Practice reading the following times.

(1) 1:15	(2) 3:25 a.m.	(3) 3:47 p.m.	(4) 4:30
(5) 6:09	(6) 8:12 a.m.	(7) 10:55 p.m.	(8) 12:36

2. Connect the corresponding words.

일	.	. 만나요
친구	.	. 해요
선물	.	. 들어요
수업	.	. 사요

GRAMMAR

G5.3 ~(으)러 [place]에 가요

Examples

(1)   A: 어디 가세요?   Where are you going?
        B: 점심 먹**으러** 한국 식당**에** 가요.   I'm going to a Korean
                                restaurant to have lunch.

(2)   A: 어디 가세요?
        B: 테니스 치**러** 가요.
        A: 테니스 좋아하세요?
        B: 네, 좋아해요.

Notes

1. [Verb~(으)러], which is parallel to English expression [(in order) to verb], is used with directional verbs 가다/오다 to indicate the purpose of going or coming.

Purpose	Destination	Directional verb
점심 먹으러	한국 식당에	가요
테니스 치러	–	가요

2. The particle 에 'to' is used to indicate destination or goal (G5.1), typically with directional verbs. As shown in the example 테니스 치러 가요, the phrase indicating destination may be omitted.

3. ~으러 is used after a verb stem ending in a consonant as in (1), while ~러 is used after a verb stem ending in a vowel as in (2).

Exercises

1. Fill in the blanks with appropriate verbs using ~(으)러.

      (1)   친구 만나러 커피숍에 가요.
      (2)   테니스 _____ 공원에 가요.
      (3)   한국어를 연습_____ 매일 컴퓨터 랩에 와요.
      (4)   점심을 _____ 학교 식당에 가요.
      (5)   이번 일요일에 옷을 _____ 옷가게에 가요.

2. Write what you would do in the following places. Then describe why you are going there.

	Place	What you do there	Full sentences
(1)	도서관	공부해요	공부하러 도서관에 가요.
(2)	커피숍		
(3)	식당		
(4)	서점		
(5)	백화점		

G5.4 Irregular verbs in /ㄷ/

Examples

(1)   A: 이번 학기에 몇 과목 **들으세요?**   How many courses are you
                                                    taking this semester?

       B: 두 과목 **들어요**.
       A: 매일 수업이 있으세요?
       B: 네. 월(요일), 수(요일), 금(요일)에는
             역사 수업이 있어요. 그리고 화(요일),
             목(요일)에는 정치학을 **들어요**.

(2)   A: 어디 가세요?
       B: 공원에 **걸으러** 가요.

Note

1. While most verb stems do not change, some verbs are subject to variation depending on the following sound. These verbs are called irregular verbs. For example, verbs 듣다 and 걷다 have /ㄷ/ at the end of the stem, and this /ㄷ/ changes to /ㄹ/ when followed by a vowel, as shown below.

듣 + 어요   →   들어요   걷 + 어요   →   걸어요
듣 + 으세요   →   들으세요   걷 + 으세요   →   걸으세요

Exercise

1. Fill in the blanks with the appropriate verb forms.

	들어요	
걷다		걸으세요

Narration   생일 선물

이번 토요일이 제 친구 스티브 생일이에요. 그래서 오늘 생일
선물을 사러 백화점에 가요. 소피아하고 같이 가요. 백화점
안에는 커피숍, 식당, 옷가게, 서점이 있어요. 1층에 서점하고
커피숍이 있어요. 2층에는 옷가게가 있어요. 그리고 3층에는
식당이 있어요. 스티브가 책을 아주 좋아해요. 그래서 저는
서점에 책을 사러 가요. 소피아는 옷가게에 옷을 사러 가요.
옷가게 옷이 아주 예뻐요.

Exercises

1. Fill in the blanks based on the narration.

    (1)   이번 토요일이 스티브 _____이에요.

    (2)   백화점에 _____하고 같이 가요.

    (3)   백화점 안에 _____, _____, _____, _____이/가 있어요.

    (4)   스티브는 책을 사러 _____에 가요.

    (5)   소피아는 옷을 사러 _____ 에 가요.

2. Ask your classmate the following questions.

    (1)   어디서 쇼핑을 해요?   (2)   어디서 옷을 사요?

    (3)   어디서 친구를 만나요?   (4)   어디서 공부해요?

3. Write the appropriate Korean sentences for the underlined English translation.

이번 토요일이 제 친구 스티브 생일이에요. 그래서 오늘 (1) I go to the department store to buy Steve's birthday present. 소피하고 같이 가요. 3시 30분에 (2) I meet Sophia in front of the dormitory. 백화점 안에는 커피숍, 식당, 옷가게, 서점이 있어요. 1층에 서점하고 커피숍이 있어요. 2층에는 옷가게가 있어요. 그리고 3층에는 식당이 있어요. (3) Steve likes books a lot. 그래서 (4) I'm going to the bookstore to buy a book. (5) Sophia's going to the clothing store to buy some clothes. 옷가게 옷이 아주 예뻐요.

    (1)   _____

    (2)   _____

    (3)   _____

    (4)   _____

    (5)   _____

CULTURE

생일 미역국 (Seaweed soup for birthday)

Seaweed soup is a traditional birthday dish for breakfast in Korea. On someone's birthday, Koreans ask "Did you have seaweed soup?" to greet the birthday person.

It is also the most popular dish among new mothers. Korean women usually eat this soup for at least three weeks after giving birth. Since seaweed soup is rich in calcium and iodine, it's effective in contracting the uterus and stopping bleeding, so it helps in recovery after childbirth. Naturally low in calories and fat, it is a light and healthy soup. However, Koreans would not eat this soup on an exam day because seaweed is slippery and gives the idea of failing an exam. Thus Koreans say "I had seaweed soup!" when they fail an exam.

USAGE

A. Saying good-bye

Remember that, in saying good-bye, location must be taken into account.

A is at home, B is leaving	A and B are saying good-bye on the street.
A: 안녕히 가세요. B: 안녕히 계세요.	A: 안녕히 가세요. B: 안녕히 가세요.

[Exercise] Exchange greetings that are appropriate for the given context with your partner.

> (1)   General greeting.
>
> (2)   Introducing two of your friends to each other.
>
> (3)   Meeting someone after a long while.
>
> (4)   You are departing from your partner's place.
>
> (5)   You are seeing your partner off on the street.

B. Asking and telling about destination and purpose

[Exercise] Practice as in the example.

> (1)   A: 어디 가세요?
>
>   B: [선물, 백화점] 선물 사러 백화점에 가요.
>
> (2)   A: 어디 가세요?
>
>   B: [옷, 옷가게] _____

(3)　　A:　　어디 가세요?

　　　　B:　　[점심, 학교 식당] _____

(4)　　A:　　어디 가세요?

　　　　B:　　[햄버거, 식당] _____

(5)　　A:　　어디 가세요?

　　　　B:　　[커피, 커피숍] _____

C. Coming and going: 가다/오다

The same motion may be described differently depending on whether the movement is toward or away from the speaker.

1. Both A and B are at the destination (e.g., school), and actions move toward both speakers.

　　　　A:　　학교에 매일 와요?
　　　　B:　　네, 매일 와요

2. Neither A nor B is at the destination, and actions move away from both speakers.

　　　　A:　　어디 가세요?
　　　　B:　　학교에 가요.
　　　　　　　학교에 가세요?
　　　　A:　　아니요, 저는 집에 가요.

3. In telephone conversation: A is at school and B is at home.

　　　　A:　　오늘 학교에 오세요?
　　　　B:　　네, 가요.
　　　　　　　오후에 시험이 있어요.

'Movement' away from speaker	'Movement' toward speaker
[Place]에 가다	[Place]에 오다

[Exercises]

(1)   (Both Jenny and Michael are at school.)

제니: 마이클 씨, 내일은 학교에 몇 시에 _____?

마이클: 8시 40분에 _____

(2)   (Sophia and Yumi are talking on the phone about Lisa's birthday
       party tonight.)

소피아: 유미 씨, 오늘 리사 생일 파티에 _____?

유미: 네, 가요. 소피아 씨도 _____?

소피아: 네, 저도 가요.

(3)   (Lisa calls Sophia to ask what time she will come to the party.)

리사: 소피아 씨, 파티에 몇 시에 _____?

소피아: 6시에 _____

D. Asking and telling about time

1.   A: 지금 몇 시예요?
      B: 10시 24분 (열 시 이십사 분)이에요.

2.   A: 지금 몇 시예요?
      B: 8시 30분이에요.

[Exercise] Based on the given context, create a dialogue with your partner.

(1)   What time is your Korean class?
              A: 한국어 수업이 몇 시에 있어요?
              B: 1시에 있어요.

(2)   What time do you come to school?

(3)   What time do you eat breakfast?

(4)   What time is it now?

(5)   What time do you go to bed?

Lesson 5 At the Bookstore

CONVERSATION 1: I'm meeting a friend at the bookstore.

Jenny:	Hi, Lisa!
Lisa:	Oh, hi, Jenny. It's been a long time.
Jenny:	Yes, it's been a long while. (By the way,) where are you going?
Lisa:	I'm going to the cafe.
	Where are you going, Jenny?
Jenny:	I'm going to the bookstore. My friend works at the bookstore across the campus.
Lisa:	Oh, really? Okay, I'll see you at school tomorrow.
Jenny:	Okay, good-bye.

CONVERSATION 2: I'm going to the department store to buy a gift.

Sophia:	Michael, what are you doing today?
Michael:	I'm going to the department store to buy a birthday gift for my friend.
Sophia:	When is it?
Michael:	This Saturday. Sophia, what are you doing today?
Sophia:	I'm going to school for my morning class.
Michael:	What time is your class?
Sophia:	At ten o'clock.
Michael:	Then let's go to the department store together in the afternoon.
Sophia:	Okay, sounds good.
Michael:	Three thirty is okay for you?
Sophia:	Yes, it's okay.

Narration: Birthday gift

This Saturday is my friend Steve's birthday, so I'm going to the department store today to buy a gift for him. Sophia is going with me. The department store has a coffee shop, a restaurant, clothing stores, and a bookstore. The first floor has the bookstore and coffee shop. The second floor has the clothing store. The third floor has the restaurant. Steve enjoys reading very much, so I'm going to the bookstore to buy him a book. Sophia's going to the clothing store to buy some clothes for herself. The clothing store carries very beautiful outfits.

6과 나의 하루 [My Day]

마이클: 제니 씨, 어디 살아요?

제니: 한인타운에 살아요.

마이클: 집에서 학교까지 얼마나 걸려요?

제니: 차로[G6.1] 한 시간쯤 걸려요.

  마이클 씨도 집에서 학교까지 멀어요?

마이클: 아니요, 아주 가까워요.[G6.2]

  저는 학교 앞 아파트에 살아요.

  보통 걸어서 10분 걸려요.

NEW WORDS

NOUN		VERB	
날씨	weather	걸리다(걸려요)	to take [time]
말(하다)	speech, words	살다(살아요)	to live
버스	bus	쓰다	to write
볼펜	ball point pen	ADJECTIVE	
비행기	airplane	가깝다(가까워요)	to be close, near
연필	pencil	덥다	to be hot
자전거	bicycle	멀다(멀어요)	to be far
지하철	subway	쉽다	to be easy
차	car	어렵다	to be difficult
하루	(one) day	춥다	to be cold
한인타운	Korea town	좁다	to be narrow
PARTICLE		ADVERB	
까지	up to (location)	보통	usually
(으)로	① by means of	얼마나/얼마	how long/how much
에서	② from (location)	조금	a little
SUFFIX		COUNTER	
쯤	about, around	시간	② hour (duration)

NEW EXPRESSIONS

1. [place A]에서 [place B]까지 'from [place A] to [place B]':

> 집에서 학교까지   from home to school
> 서울에서 보스톤까지   from Seoul to Boston

2. 쯤 is an expression of approximate quantity and quality, best translated as 'about' or 'around'. It is usually attached to a noun expressing time or number.

3. In asking about someone's residence, you may ask 어디 살아요/사세요? 'Where do you live?' or 집이 어디예요/어디세요? 'Where is your home?' (see lesson 4, conversation 1).

     As in [place]에 살아요 and [place]에서 살아요, from the examples below, 살다 'to live' may take either the static locative particle 에 or the dynamic locative particle 에서. The difference in meaning is very subtle and hardly noticeable.

> 학교 아파트에 살아요.   =   학교 아파트에서 살아요.
> 캠퍼스 밖에 살아요.   =   캠퍼스 밖에서 살아요. (밖 'outside')

4. ~어서/아서 is attached to verbs like 걷다 'walk', 뛰다 'run', or 운전하다 'drive'

to express means of motion: 걸어서, 뛰어서, 운전해서.

마이클은 집에서 학교까지 걸어서 가요.

5. Expressions of frequency:

매일/날마다	every day	매주	every week
매일 아침	every morning	매달	every month
매일 저녁	every evening	매년	every year

Exercises

1. Create questions and answers using either 가깝다 or 멀다 as in the example.

(1)   [교실, 도서관]   교실에서 도서관까지 멀어요?

네, 멀어요.

(2)   [서점, 식당]   _____?

네, _____

(3)   [기숙사, 도서관]   _____?

아니요, _____

(4)   [컴퓨터 랩, 교실]   _____?

네, _____

(5)   [집, 백화점]   _____?

아니요, _____

(6)   [학교, 우체국]   _____?

아니요, _____

2. Ask your classmates the following questions, and find out who lives the farthest away from school.

A: 어디 살아요?

B: _____에/에서 살아요.

A: 집에서 학교까지 얼마나 걸려요?

B: _____시간(분) 걸려요.

3. Complete the following sentences.

(1)   매일 공원에서 운동해요.

(2) 매주 _____

(3) 매달 _____

(4) 매년 _____

GRAMMAR

G6.1 N(으)로 'by means of N'

Examples

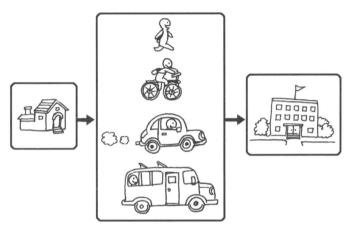

[transportation]

(1) A: 학교에 차**로** 가요?
    B: 저는 차가 없어요.
       버스**로** 가요.

(2) A: 학교에 걸어서 가요?
    B: 아니요, 차**로** 가요.

(3) A: 학교에 어떻게 가요?
    B: 자전거**로** 가요.

[instrument]

(4) 한국어**로** 말하세요.　　　　　Please speak in Korean.

(5) 볼펜**으로** 쓰세요.　　　　　Please write with a ballpoint pen.

Notes

1. Means of transportation is expressed with the particle (으)로. 으로 is used after a noun ending in a consonant (except /ㄹ/), and 로 is used after a noun ending in a vowel and a consonant /ㄹ/.

비행기로	by airplane	차로	by car
트럭으로	by truck	지하철로	by subway

2. The particle (으)로 is also used to indicate an instrument by means of which an action is performed.

영어로	in English	연필로	with a pencil

Exercises

1. How do you come to school?

    (1)   [by bicycle]   자전거로 와요. ___

    (2)   [by bus]   _____

    (3)   [by walking]   _____

    (4)   [by subway]   _____

    (5)   [by car]   _____

2. What kind of action do you perform with the items within the brackets?

    (1)   [볼펜]   볼펜으로 이름을 써요. ___

    (2)   [영어]   _____

    (3)   [연필]   _____

    (4)   [한국어]   _____

G6.2 Irregular predicates in /ㅂ/

Examples

(1)   A: 한인타운에서 학교까지 멀어요?
        B: 아니요, **가까워요**.

(2)   A: 한국어 시험이 **쉬워요**?
        B: 아니요, 조금 **어려워요**.

Note

1. Some predicates whose stem ends in /ㅂ/ are subject to variation in the stem form. When the following suffix begins with a vowel (e.g., ~어요/아요, ~(으)세요), /ㅂ/ becomes 우. That is, /ㅂ/ → 우 before a vowel:

가깝다: 가**깝** + 어요/아요   → 가**까우** + 어요*   → 가**까워**요 (우 + 어 = 워)

가**깝** + 으세요   → 가**까우** + 으세요 → 가**까우**세요 (우 + 으 = 우)

*The dark vowel 우 cannot be combined with a bright vowel 아, and therefore, ~어요 is used instead of ~아요.

가깝다	춥다	어렵다
가까워요	추워요	어려워요

For all irregular predicates in /ㅂ/, the stem final 우, and the vowel 어 of the polite ending ~어요 must be contracted. Notice that the regular verb 좁다 becomes 좁아요.

가깝다 가깝→ 가까우 가까**우** + **어**요 → 가까**워**요	좁다 좁 좁 + 아요 → 좁아요

Exercises

1. Fill in the boxes with appropriate forms of predicates.

~어요/아요	추워요	가까워요		쉬워요	
~(으)세요			더우세요		좁으세요

2. Fill in the blanks with the proper form of the given predicate.

    (1)   이번 숙제는 <u>쉬워요</u> (쉽다).

    (2)   A: 요즘 한국 날씨가 어때요?

            B: 아주 _____ (춥다) .

    (3)   A: 아파트에서 공원까지 멀어요?

            B: 아니요, _____ (가깝다).

    (4)   A: 정치학 재미있어요?

            B: 네, 재미있어요.

                 그런데 조금 _____ (어렵다).

    (5)   학생: 선생님, 지금 _____ (덥다)?

            선생님: 아니요, 괜찮아요.

Conversation 2 | 어제 뭐 했어요?

마이클: 유미 씨, 어제 오후에 뭐 했어요?^G6.3

유미: 학교 수영장에서 수영했어요.

           마이클 씨는 뭐 했어요?

마이클: 친구하고 같이 테니스 쳤어요.

유미: 아, 제니하고 쳤어요?

마이클: 아니요, 제니는 테니스 안^G6.4 좋아해요.

           유미 씨는 테니스 좋아해요?

유미: 네, 그런데 잘 못^G6.4 쳐요.

NEW WORDS

NOUN		ADJECTIVE	
수영(하다)	swimming	바쁘다	to be busy
수영장	swimming pool	**ADVERB**	
어제	yesterday	너무	too much
음악	music	못	cannot
전화(하다)	telephone	안	do not
주말	weekend	왜	why
테니스장	tennis court		
파티	party	**PRE-NOUN**	
VERB		지난	last, past
모르다	to not know, be unaware of	**SUFFIX**	
일어나다	to get up	~었/았/ㅆ	past tense

NEW EXPRESSIONS

In describing one's ability, the following expressions are often used:
잘 해요 'good at, skillful at'; 못 해요 'bad at, unskillful at'; 잘 못 해요 'not that good at'.

Exercises

1. Find out who can play tennis and who cannot among your classmates.

2. Find out who can swim and who cannot among your classmates.

3. Connect the opposite words.

넓어요   ·   ·   더워요

추워요   ·   ·   없어요

있어요   ·   ·   가까워요

멀어요   ·   ·   좁아요

GRAMMAR

G6.3 Past events:~었/았/ㅆ어요

Examples

(1)   A: 스티브 어디 **갔어요**?
       B: 집에 **갔어요**.

(2)   A: 일요일 오전에 뭐 **했어요**?
       B: 형하고 같이 운동**했어요**.

(3)   A: 오늘 점심 어**땠어요**?
       B: 괜찮**았어요**.

(4)   지난 주말에 학교 테니스장에서 친구를 **만났어요.**

(5)   오늘 8시에 아침을 먹**었어요**.

Notes

1. ~었/았/ㅆ indicates that the event described has already taken place.

2. Selecting the correct past tense form among the three variants follows the same principle as for choosing between ~어요 and ~아요 (G2.5): (i) ~았어요 when the last vowel of the stem is either 아 or 오, and (ii) ~었어요 elsewhere. (iii) ~ㅆ어요 is used when vowel contractions occur (G4.5) as in 갔어요. The final ending after ~었/았/ㅆ is always ~어요, not ~아요.

많다	많아요	좋다	좋아요
	많았어요		좋았어요
일어나다	일어나요	오다	와요
	일어났어요		왔어요
먹다	먹어요	맛있다	맛있어요
	먹었어요		맛있었어요
배우다	배워요	전화하다	전화해요
	배웠어요		전화했어요
이다	이에요/예요	아니다	아니에요
	이었어요/였어요		아니었어요

3. Verbs and adjectives whose stems end in 으 have the following forms.

쓰다	써요	크다	커요
	썼어요		컸어요
바쁘다	바빠요	예쁘다	예뻐요
	바빴어요		예뻤어요

Exercises

1. Give the proper form of the past tense.

    (1)   오늘 7시 30에 아침을 <u>먹었어요</u>(먹다).

    (2)   A: 어제 오후에 뭐 했어요?

            B: _____ (수영하다).

    (3)   A: 어제 뭐 했어요?

            B: 백화점에서 _____ (쇼핑하다).

    (4)   A: 지난 주말에 뭐 했어요?

            B: 친구를 _____ (만나다).

    (5)   A: 지난 학기가 어땠어요?

            B: _____ (바쁘다).

    (6)   저는 보통 7시에 일어나요.
            그런데 오늘은 8시에 _____ (일어나다).

2. Ask your partner the following questions in Korean.

    (1)   What did you eat for dinner yesterday?

    (2)   What did you do last weekend?

    (3)   How many hours did you sleep yesterday?

    (4)   What time did you get up this morning?

    (5)   What time did you come to school today?

G6.4   The negative adverb 안 vs. 못

Examples

(1)   제니: 마이클 씨는 학교에 매일 와요?
       마이클: 아니요. 화요일하고 목요일에는 **안** 와요.

(2)   마이클: 유미 씨, 수영장 가세요?
       유미: 아니요, 도서관에 가요. 오늘은 수영 **못** 해요.

(3)   (Steve didn't come to the party yesterday. Jenny calls him to find out why.)
       제니: 스티브 씨,   Steve, why didn't you come
                     왜 파티에 **안** 왔어요?   to the party?
       스티브: 바빴어요.   I was busy.
                     그래서 **못** 갔어요.   And so I could not go.

Notes

1. Negation of a predicate in general is made by putting the negative adverb 안 or 못 immediately before the predicate.

	Do not	Cannot
가요	**안** 가요	**못** 가요
먹어요	**안** 먹어요	**못** 먹어요

안 is used for general negation, 못 'cannot' is used when external circumstances prevent a person from doing something. As in example (3), in English you can say "I didn't go because I was busy," but in Korean, you have to say 못 갔어요 (not 안 갔어요). Also note that 안 occurs only with a subject with its own volition.

2. Negation of [N + 하다] verbs is usually made by putting 안 or 못 between the noun and the verb 하다, that is, [N 안 하다] or [N 못 하다], as in the following examples.

N 하다	N 안 하다	N 못 하다
전화-해요	전화 **안** 해요	전화 **못** 해요
일-해요	일 **안** 해요	일 **못** 해요

3. Some verbs and adjectives have a special negative counterpart. For these predicates, the regular negative construction with 안/못 is not used.

Positive	Negative
있다 (있어요)	없다 (없어요)
맛있다 (맛있어요)	맛없다 (맛없어요)
이다 (이에요)	아니다 (아니에요)
알다 (알아요)	모르다 (몰라요)

Exercises

1. Give a negative answer to the question.

    (1)   A: 매일 아침을 먹어요?

              B: 아니요, 보통 안 <u>먹어요</u>.

    (2)   A: 매일 운동하세요?

              B: 아니요, 토요일, 일요일에는 _____

    (3)   A: 오늘 학교에 가요?

              B: 아니요, _____

                    오늘 수업이 _____

    (4)   A: 파티가 재미있었어요?

              B: 아니요, _____

    (5)   A: 스티브 씨, 제임스 알아요?

              B: 아니요, _____

2. Fill in the blanks with either 안 or 못, based on the context.

    (1)   A: 오늘 리사 생일 파티에 가요?

              B: 내일 오전에 시험이 있어요. 그래서 못 가요.

    (2)   A: 한국어 숙제 했어요?

              B: 아니요, _____ 했어요. 너무 어려워요.

    (3)   A: 클래식 ('classic') 음악 좋아하세요?

              B: 아니요, _____ 좋아해요.

    (4)   A: 어제 정치학 시험 잘 봤어요?

              B: 아니요, 잘 _____ 봤어요.

Narration   마이클의 하루

저는 보통 7시에 일어나요. 그런데 오늘은 8시 30분에
일어났어요. 그래서 아침을 못 먹었어요. 수업은 9시에
있었어요. 기숙사에서 학교까지는 가까워요. 그래서 보통
걸어서 가요. 오후에는 수업이 없었어요. 그래서, 리사하고
테니스를 쳤어요. 리사는 제 여자 친구예요. 리사도 한국어
수업을 들어요. 6시쯤 리사하고 같이 저녁을 먹으러 기숙사
식당에 갔어요. 그리고 저녁에는 도서관에서 숙제를 했어요.
숙제가 어려웠어요. 오늘 하루는 아주 바빴어요.

Exercises

1. Tell your classmate what you did since you woke up this morning.

저는 오늘 7시에 일어났어요. 그리고 8시에 . . .

2. Read the narration and answer the following questions.

(1)   마이클은 오늘 몇 시에 일어났어요?
(2)   마이클은 오늘 왜 아침을 못 먹었어요?
(3)   학교에 어떻게 가요?
(4)   오후에 뭐 했어요?
(5)   리사가 누구예요?
(6)   저녁 먹으러 어디에 갔어요?
(7)   저녁에 왜 도서관에 갔어요?

3. Change the predicates in the parentheses into the past form.

저는 보통 7시에 일어나요. 그런데 오늘은 8시 30분에 _____(일어나다).
그래서 아침을 못 _____ (먹다). 수업은 9시에 _____ (있다).
기숙사에서 학교까지는 가까워요. 그래서 보통 걸어서 가요. 오후에는 수업이
_____ (없다). 그래서, 리사하고 테니스를 _____ (치다). 리사는
제 여자 친구예요. 리사도 한국어 수업을 들어요. 6시쯤 리사하고 같이 저녁을
먹으러 기숙사 식당에 _____ (가다). 그리고 저녁에는 도서관에서
숙제를 _____ (하다). 숙제가 _____ (어렵다). 오늘 하루는 아주
_____ (바쁘다).

CULTURE

1. 달력 'calendar'

Koreans reckon days according to both the solar and lunar calendars. The solar
calendar is called 양(Yang)력 and the lunar calendar 음(Yin)력. Most national
holidays are observed based on the solar calendar. However, New Year's Day
(설날) is celebrated according to both calendars, while the Moon Festival (추석) is
observed on August 15th of the lunar calendar, which usually falls in September.

2. Writing dates: 2012년 10월 28일

In Korean, dates are written from the largest unit to the smallest, that is, year first, followed by month and day. Thus, October 28, 2012, is read in Korean as 2012년 (이천 십이 년) 10월 (시 월) 28일 (이십팔 일). Similarly, in identifying a person's academic status, the university is named first, the major or department next, and the school year last, as in 뉴욕 대학(교) 생물학과 4학년 'a senior in the department of biology at New York University'. Addresses are also written from largest unit to smallest with the person's name at the end.

USAGE

A. Talking about how much time something takes

A: 집에서 학교까지 얼마나 걸려요?

B: (i)   걸어서 30분 걸려요.
       (ii)   차로 5분 걸려요.
       (iii)   자전거로 15분 걸려요.
       (iv)   버스로 1시간 걸려요.

As shown above, [time] 걸리다 specifies how long (how much time) some action or activity takes.

[Exercise] How long does it take to go from your place to school?

(1)   A: 집에서 학교까지 얼마나 걸려요?
       B: [by subway, 50 minutes] 지하철로 오십 분 걸려요.
(2)   [by car, 20 minutes]   _____
(3)   [by bicycle, 1 hour]   _____
(4)   [by bus, 45 minutes]   _____
(5)   [by walking, 5 minutes]   _____

B. Talking about habitual and past activities

[Exercise] Interview your classmates and find out about their habitual activities and past events.

Day	Habitual activities: ~어요/아요 질문: 보통 월요일에 뭐 해요?	Past events: ~었어요/았어요/써어요 질문: 지난 월요일에 뭐 했어요?
월요일		
화요일		
수요일		
목요일		
금요일		
토요일		
일요일		

C. Talking about daily activities

[Exercise 1] The following is Steve's daily schedule for this semester. Answer the following questions based on the schedule.

	월요일	화요일	수요일	목요일	금요일
9:00~10:00					
10:00~11:00	음악 350 존슨홀		음악 350 존슨홀		음악 350 존슨홀
11:00~12:00		컴퓨터 110 웨스트홀		컴퓨터 110 웨스트홀	
12:00~1:00	점심	점심	점심	점심	점심
1:00~2:00	한국어 101 이스트홀	한국어 101 이스트홀	한국어 101 이스트홀	한국어 101 이스트홀	한국어 101 이스트홀
2:00~3:00					
3:00~4:00			한국어 랩 이스트홀		
4:00~5:00		생물학 120 무어홀		생물학 120 무어홀	

(1)   스티브는 매일 학교에 와요? _____

(2)   한국어 수업은 언제 있어요? _____

       한국어 수업은 어디서 해요? _____

(3)   수요일 10시 수업은 뭐예요? _____

(4)   화, 목은 몇 시에 수업이 끝나요 ('to end')? _____

(5)   한국어 랩은 언제 들어요? _____

       한국어 랩은 어디서 해요? _____

(6)   점심은 몇 시에 먹어요? _____

(7)   스티브는 이번 학기에 몇 과목 들어요? 뭐 들어요?

       _____

[Exercise 2] Make your own timetable, and describe your daily schedule.

[Exercise 3] Answer the questions based on Michael's daily schedule below.

7:00	일어나다	
8:00	아침을 먹다	기숙사 식당
8:40	기숙사에서 나오다 ('to come out')	
8:50	학교에 오다	걸어서
9:00	한국어 수업	월, 화, 수 목, 금
3:00	테니스 치다	리사하고
6:30	저녁을 먹다	학교 식당
7:00	공부하다	도서관
10:20	집에 가다	
11:00	자다	

(1)   마이클은 몇 시에 일어나요? _____

(2)   마이클은 어디서 아침을 먹어요? _____

(3)   기숙사에서 학교까지 얼마나 걸려요? _____

(4)   학교에 어떻게 가요? _____

(5)   한국어 수업은 몇 시에 있어요? _____

(6)   한국어 수업은 매일 있어요? _____

(7)   오후에는 뭐 해요? _____

(8)   마이클은 어디서 저녁을 먹어요? _____

(9)   저녁에는 뭐 해요? _____

(10)   마이클은 몇 시간 공부해요? _____

(11)   마이클은 몇 시간 자요? _____

D. Asking reasons: 왜 'why?'

A: **왜** 한국어를 공부하세요?
B: 한국 친구가 많아요.

[Exercise] Make up dialogues that are appropriate for the given context with your partner.

> Example: Michael is busy because he is taking five courses this semester.
>
> 유미: 마이클 씨, 요즘 어떻게 지내세요?
> 마이클: 조금 바빠요.
> 유미: 왜요?
> 마이클: 수업이 많아요.

(1) The school cafeteria is usually not a favorite place for lunch. But Lisa likes to have lunch at the school cafeteria because the coffee is good.

유미: 리사 씨는 점심 어디서 먹어요?
리사: _____
유미: _____ Any particular reason?
리사: _____

(2) Michael is going to a department store to buy a gift for his parents.

유미: 마이클 씨, 어디 가세요?
마이클: _____
유미: _____ Why?
마이클: _____

(3) Yumi is asking some questions of Steve, who studies Korean.

유미: 스티브 씨, 뭐 공부하세요?

스티브: _____

유미: _____

          Why do you study Korean?

스티브: _____

(4) Interview three of your classmates and find out why they are studying Korean.

          Examples

          한국어가 재미있어요.   Korean is fun.

          한국 친구가 많아요.   I have many Korean friends.

          한국 음식을 좋아해요.   I like Korean food.

          한국을 좋아해요.   I like Korea.

          제 전공이 한국 문학/역사예요.   My major is Korean literature/
                                                  history.

Lesson 6 My Day

CONVERSATION 1: It takes about an hour by car.

Michael:	Where do you live, Jenny?
Jenny:	I live in Koreatown.
Michael:	How long does it take from your home to get to school?
Jenny:	It takes about an hour by car. Do you live far from school as well?
Michael:	No, I live close by. I live in the apartment across campus. It usually takes ten minutes to walk.

CONVERSATION 2: What did you do yesterday?

Michael:	Yumi, what did you do yesterday afternoon?
Yumi:	I swam in the school swimming pool. What did you do, Michael?
Michael:	I played tennis with a friend.
Yumi:	Oh, did you play with Jenny?
Michael:	No, she doesn't like tennis. Yumi, do you like to play tennis?
Yumi:	Yes, but I don't know how to play tennis very well.

NARRATION: Michael's day

I usually get up at seven o'clock in the morning, but today I got up at eight thirty and didn't have breakfast. I have class at nine o'clock. My dorm is close to campus. I usually walk to school. Since I don't have any class in the afternoon, I played tennis with Lisa. Lisa is my girlfriend. She also takes the Korean class. Around six o'clock, Lisa and I went to the dormitory cafeteria to have dinner. In the evening, I did my homework at the library alone. The homework was difficult. Today was a very busy day.

7과 주말 [The Weekend]

Conversation 1 | 친구하고 영화 볼 거예요.

(Steve and Lisa talk about their weekend plans.)

스티브: 리사 씨, 어제 경제학 시험 잘 봤어요?

리사: 네, 잘 봤어요. 그런데 시험이 조금 어려웠어요.

　　　 참, 스티브 씨, 이번 주말에 약속 있으세요?

스티브: 아니요, 없어요.

리사: 저는 친구하고 영화 볼 거예요. G7.1

　　　 스티브 씨도 같이 가요.

스티브: 무슨G7.2 영화 볼 거예요?

리사: 액션 영화요.

스티브: 그럼 같이 가요.

　　　 보통 어느 극장에 자주 가세요?

리사: 브로드웨이 극장에 자주 가요.

NEW WORDS

NOUN		영화	movie
계절	season	이스트 홀	East Hall
꽃	flower	코미디	comedy
극장	movie theater	**VERB**	
나라	country	받다	to receive
내년	next year	**ADVERB**	
다음	next, following	아마	probably, perhaps
대학원	graduate school	자주	often, frequently
방학	school vacation	정말	really
브로드웨이 극장	Broadway theater	참	② by the way
약속	① engagement;	**PRE-NOUN**	
	② promise	무슨	what, what kind of
액션 영화	action movie	어느	which
여름	summer	**SUFFIX**	
여행(하다)	travel	~(으)ㄹ 거예요	probability

NEW EXPRESSIONS

1. 참 'by the way' is often used when one comes to remember something to say.

2. Time expressions: days, weeks, months, and years:

지난		이번		다음	
지난 월요일	last Monday	이번 월요일	this Monday	다음 월요일	next Monday
지난 토요일	last Saturday	이번 토요일	this Saturday	다음 토요일	next Saturday
지난 주말	last weekend	이번 주말	this weekend	다음 주말	next weekend
지난 주	last week	이번 주	this week	다음 주	next week
지난 달	last month	이(번) 달	this month	다음 달	next month
작년	last year	올해	this year	내년	next year

Exercises

1. Fill in the blanks based on conversation 1.

     (1)   리사는 이번 주말에 _____를 볼 거예요.

     (2)   스티브는 이번 주말에 _____이 없어요.

     (3)   리사 씨는 _____영화를 볼 거예요.

     (4)   리사는 브로드웨이 _____에 자주 가요.

2. Write the corresponding words.

     (1)   서점: _____책_____   (2)   백화점: _____

     (3)   극장: _____   (4)   커피숍: _____

     (5)   옷가게: _____   (6)   식당: _____

GRAMMAR

G7.1 Probability: ~(으)ㄹ 거예요

Examples

(1)   소피아: 마이클 씨, 이번 방학에 뭐 **할 거예요**?

          마이클: 리사하고 하와이에 **갈 거예요.**

                      소피아 씨는 집에 있**을 거예요**?

          소피아: 홍콩에서 오빠가 와요. 그래서 오빠하고 여행**할 거예요.**

(2)   유미: 스티브 씨, 다음 학기에 몇 과목 들을 거예요?

          스티브: 네 과목 **들을 거예요.**

Note

1. ~(으)ㄹ 거예요 is an expression of probability. It marks a situation the speaker thinks is likely to happen and often expresses the speaker's or the listener's intention or plan. However, a scheduled event is often expressed in the present tense. The form ~을 거예요 is used when the verb stem ends in a consonant as in 있을 거예요; ~ㄹ 거예요 is used when the verb stem ends in a vowel as in 갈 거예요.

[intention or plan]
다음 주말에 뭐 할 거예요?   What do you plan to do next weekend?
다음 주말에 저는 영화를 볼 거예요.   I intend to see a movie next weekend.

[probable future]
다음 월요일에 시험이 있을 거예요.   There will (probably) be an exam next
                                                       Monday.

[definite future]
다음 월요일에 시험이 있어요.   There is an exam next Monday.
내일이 제 생일이에요.   Tomorrow is my birthday.

The present and future forms of some irregular verbs (see also G5.4 and G6.2) are
as shown below.

Dictionary form	~어요/아요	~(으)ㄹ 거예요
/ㄷ/ irregular: 듣다	들어요	들을 거예요 (들 + 을 거예요)
/ㅂ/ irregular: 춥다	추워요	추울 거예요 (추우 + ㄹ 거예요)

Exercise

1. Complete the following sentences appropriately with the given predicates,
using ~어요/아요, ~었어요/았어요/써어요, or ~(으)ㄹ 거예요.

(1)   A: 이번 여름에 뭐 <u>할 거예요</u> (하다)?
         B: 친구하고 수영 <u>배울 거예요</u> (배우다).

(2)   리사: 스티브 씨, 지난 주말에 뭐 _____ (하다)?
         스티브: 생일파티 _____ (하다).
                     토요일이 제 생일_____ (이다).
         리사: 아, 그랬어요? _____ (축하하다 'congratulate').
         스티브: _____ (고맙다).
                     리사 씨 생일은 언제 _____ (이다)?
         리사: 6월 27일 _____ (이다).

(3)   다음 주말에는 리사하고 뉴욕에 _____ (가다).
         뉴욕에 리사 언니가 _____ (있다).
         리사 언니는 지금 대학교 4학년_____ (이다).
         내년에 아마 대학원에 _____ (가다).

(4)   A: 어제 리사 생일 파티에 _____ (가다)?

      B: 아니요, 저녁에 친구를 _____ (만나다).

(5)   A: 다음 학기에 뭐 _____ (듣다)?

      B: 한국어하고 생물학을 _____ (듣다).

G7.2   무슨 'what (kind of) N' vs. 어느 'which N'

Examples

[무슨]

(1)   A: 생일에 **무슨** 선물을 받았어요?   What (kind of) present did
                                              you get on your birthday?
      B: 꽃을 받았어요.   I got flowers.

      (pointing to a book)
(2)   A: 이거 **무슨** 책이에요?   What kind of book is this?
      B: 한국어 교과서예요.   It's the Korean textbook.

(3)   A: 이번 일요일에 뭐 할 거예요?
      B: 영화 볼 거예요.
      A: **무슨** 영화 볼 거예요?
      B: 한국 영화 볼 거예요.

[어느]

(4)   A: 이번 토요일에 **어느** 극장에서   In which theater will you be
           영화 볼 거예요?   watching the movie this
                                               weekend?
      B: 브로드웨이 극장에서 볼 거예요.   I'll be watching it at the
                                               Broadway Theater.

(5)   A: 에드워드는 **어느** 나라 사람이에요?
      B: 영국 사람이에요.

(6)   A: **어느** 계절을 좋아하세요?
      B: 여름을 정말 좋아해요.

Notes

1. 무슨 means 'what' or 'what kind of'. It always precedes a noun.

무슨 영화	what movie	무슨 선물	what present
무슨 책	what book	무슨 과목	what subject

2. 어느 is a question word that is used in asking about a choice among a set of limited candidates available, like 'which' in English. Both 무슨 and 어느 always precede a noun.

3. 어느 can be used either with nouns or demonstratives such as 것(거) 'thing', whereas 무슨 cannot be used with 것(거).

어느 책	→	어느 것	which thing (one)
어느 가방	→	어느 것	

Exercises

1. Interview your classmates using the following questions.

    (1)   어느 나라 사람이에요?

    (2)   어느 식당에서 점심을 먹어요?

    (3)   보통 어느 백화점에서 쇼핑하세요?

    (4)   다음 학기에 무슨 과목을 들을 거예요?

    (5)   무슨 영화 좋아하세요?

2. Make up questions that are appropriate for the responses provided.

    (1)   A: 지난 주말에 뭐 했어요?

            B: 친구하고 영화 봤어요.

            A: <u>무슨 영화 봤어요?</u>

            B: 코미디 영화 봤어요.

            A: <u>어느 극장에서 봤어요?</u>

            B: 브로드웨이 극장에서 봤어요.

    (2)   A: 어디 가세요?

            B: 이번 토요일이 남자 친구 생일이에요.

                    그래서 생일 선물 사러 백화점에 가요.

            A: _____?

            B: 시어즈 ('Sears') 백화점에 가요.

(3)   스티브: 유미 씨, 이번 학기에 _____?

        유미: 한국어하고 생물학 수업을 들어요.

        스티브: 한국어 교실은 _____?
                  (In which building is the Korean class?)

        유미: 이스트 홀에 있어요.

(4)   유미: _____?
                  (What building is this?)

        리사: 이건 유니온 빌딩이에요.

        유미: 학교 식당 _____?
                  (In which building is the school cafeteria?)

        리사: 학생회관 안에 있어요.

Conversation 2　파티에 안 갈 거예요?

마이클: 소피아 씨, 다음 주말에 뭐 하세요?

소피아: 집에서 청소하고[G7.3] 음식 준비할 거예요.

마이클: 왜요?

소피아: 여동생이 뉴욕에서 와요.

마이클: 그럼, 크리스마스 파티에 안 갈 거예요?[G7.4]

소피아: 네, 아마 못 갈 거예요.

마이클: 동생을 자주 봐요?

소피아: 아니요, 자주 못 봐요.

　　　　그래서 오래간만에 이야기를 많이 할 거예요.

마이클: 아, 그래요?

　　　　그럼, 크리스마스 잘 보내세요.

NEW WORDS

NOUN		청소(하다)	cleaning
가을	autumn, fall	크리스마스	Christmas
겨울	winter	**ADJECTIVE**	
마켓	market	흐리다	to be cloudy
봄	spring	**VERB**	
설거지(하다)	dishwashing	보내다	to spend time
신문	newspaper	장(을)보다	to buy one's groceries
심리학	psychology	**ADVERB**	
이야기(하다)	talk, chat (=애기)	가끔	sometimes, occasionally
전공(하다)	major	많이	much, many
주	week	서로	each other
준비(하다)	preparation	**SUFFIX**	
		~고	and (clausal connective)

Exercises

1. Fill in the blanks with your own activities.

      (1)   보통 매일 ＿＿＿＿＿＿＿고＿＿＿＿＿＿＿어/아요.

      (2)   지난 주에 ＿＿＿＿＿＿＿고＿＿＿＿＿＿＿었/았어요.

      (3)   이번 주말에 ＿＿＿＿＿＿고＿＿＿＿＿＿(으)ㄹ 거예요.

      (4)   다음 달에 ＿＿＿＿＿＿고＿＿＿＿＿＿(으)ㄹ 거예요.

2. Fill in the spaces within the brackets with appropriate words.

      (1)   사계절: [   ] – [   ] – [   ] – [   ]

      (2)   한 주: [월] – [   ] – [   ] – [목] – [   ] – [   ] – [   ]

GRAMMAR

G7.3 The clausal connective ~고

Examples

(1)   어제는 흐리**고** 추웠어요.   It was cloudy and cold yesterday.

(2)   아침을 먹고 오전에 일했어요.   I had breakfast and then worked
                                          until noon.

(3)   우리 아파트는 넓고 싸고   My apartment is spacious, cheap,
         예쁘고 학교에서 가까워요.   lovely, and close to school.

(4)   저는 로스앤젤레스에 살고 언니는   I live in Los Angeles, and my older
         하와이에 살아요.   sister lives in Hawai'i.

Notes

1. ~고 is used to link two clauses like 'and' in English. ~고 indicates that the event
or state of clause 1 coexists with that of clause 2.

2. Clause 1 is usually not marked for any tense, especially when it is interpreted
as being within the same time frame as clause 2. For example, 어제는 흐리고
추웠어요 sounds better than 어제는 흐렸고 추웠어요.

3. ~고 can represent temporal transition meaning 'and then' as in (2).

4. [clause~고] may be used more than once in a sentence, as shown in
example (3).

5. The two events or states in clause 1 and clause 2 may sometimes stand in
contrast to each other, as in example (4) above.

6. Both 하고 and ~고 are translated into 'and' in English. However, the particle
하고 is used to link two nouns (e.g., 신문하고 책 'a newspaper and a book'),
whereas ~고 links two clauses.

                          Clause 1   Clause 2
       [언니**하고** 오빠는 기숙사에 살**고**] [저는 아파트에 살아요.]
        N1   N2

Exercises

1. Combine the two sentences using ~고, as shown in the example.

(1)   저는 음악을 **전공해요. 그리고** 제 동생은 심리학을 전공해요.
         <u>저는 음악을 **전공하고** 제 동생은 심리학을 전공해요.</u>

(2)   유미는 1학년이에요. 그리고 소피아는 2학년이에요.

_____

(3)   누나는 음식을 준비했어요. 그리고 형은 설거지했어요.

_____

(4)   로스앤젤레스는 아주 커요. 그리고 사람이 많아요.

_____

(5)   저는 이번 가을 학기에 세 과목을 들어요. 그리고 봄 학기에는 네 과목을 들어요.

_____

2. Translate the following expressions into Korean using 하고 or ~고.

(1)   I bought flowers <u>and</u> books.
(2)   There was a newspaper <u>and</u> an umbrella on the desk.
(3)   My younger brother will swim, <u>and</u> I will play tennis.
(4)   Steve's major is music, <u>and</u> Michael's major is psychology.

3. Answer the following questions using ~고.

(1)   저녁 먹고 보통 뭐 하세요?

_____

(2)   지난 겨울 방학에 뭐 했어요?

_____

(3)   어제 저녁 집에서 뭐 했어요?

_____

(4)   다음 주에 뭐 할 거예요?

_____

G7.4   Negative questions

Examples

(1)   스티브: 리사 씨, 이번 주말에 뭐 할 거예요?
       리사: 오래간만에 언니하고 전화할 거예요.
       스티브: 언니하고 전화 자주 **안** 하세요?
       리사: **네**, 자주 못 해요.   [agree with the question]

(2)   스티브: 리사 씨, 무슨 선물 받았어요?
      리사: 시계하고 옷을 받았어요.

      스티브: 꽃은 **안** 받았어요?
      리사: **아니요**, 꽃도 받았어요.   [disagree with the question]

Note

1. In English, yes/no mean positive and negative realization of the events or states of affairs at issue, respectively, regardless of whether the question is asked positively or negatively. In Korean, however, 네/아니요 refers to whether the content of the question is true or false (the responder agrees or disagrees with it), respectively. Therefore, when a question is asked negatively, 네 means that the content of the question is true (or the speaker agrees with it), as in (1), and 아니요 means that the content of the question is false (or the speaker does not agree with it), as in (2).

English: A: Aren't you coming?
           B: No (I'm not coming).

Korean: A: 안 와요?   Aren't you coming?
           B: 네 (안 가요).   Yes (I'm not coming).

Exercise

1. Fill in the blanks with 네 or 아니요 based on the context.

(1)   A: 집에서 학교까지 안 가까워요?
      B: <u>아니요</u>, 가까워요.

(2)   A: 8과 안 배웠어요?
      B: _____, 안 배웠어요.

(3)   A: 마켓에 장보러 안 갈 거예요?
      B: _____, 갈 거예요.

(4)   A: 이번 학기에 전공 수업 안 들어요?
      B: _____, 들어요.

(5)   A: 극장에 자주 안 가요?
      B: _____, 자주 못 가요. 가끔 가요.

CULTURE

National holidays in Korea

1월 1일   (both solar and lunar): New Year's Day (설)

3월 1일   March First Independence Movement Day (3·1절)

4월 8일   (lunar calendar): Buddha's Birthday (석가 탄신일)

5월 5월   Children's Day (어린이 날)

6월 6일   Memorial Day (현충일)

8월 15일   Liberation Day (광복절)

8월 15일   (lunar calendar): Harvest Festival 추석 (lit. autumn evening)

10월 3일   Foundation Day (개천절)

12월 25일 Christmas (성탄절)

New Year's Day (lunar) involves big traditional celebrations. People dress in Korean clothes (한복) and make deep sitting bows (세배) to their elder relatives and acquaintances, saying 새해 복 많이 받으세요 'Receive lots of blessings in the New Year'. Children receive money called 세뱃돈 'money for the New Year's bow' after each bow. People eat a rice-cake soup called 떡국. To celebrate the Harvest Festival (추석), many people go to their hometown and pay their respects to their ancestors by visiting the ancestors' graves. Special foods are prepared using newly harvested grains and produce.

Narration   소피아의 주말

지난 주에는 시험이 많았어요. 그래서 아주 바빴어요. 주말에는
친구들하고 같이 영화를 보러 갔어요. 영화가 참 재미있었어요.
영화를 보고 중국 음식을 먹었어요. 다음 주말에는 여동생이
뉴욕에서 올 거예요. 동생은 다음 학기에 대학에 가요. 심리학을
전공할 거예요. 동생도 저도 많이 바빠요. 그래서 서로 전화를
자주 못 해요. 이번에 동생하고 오래간만에 이야기를 많이 할
거예요. 동생이 한국 음식을 좋아해요. 그래서 집에서 한국
음식을 준비할 거예요.

Exercises

1. Fill in the blanks based on the narration.

    (1)   지난 주에는 _____이 많았어요.

    (2)   주말에는 _____하고 영화를 보러 갔어요.

    (3)   _____주말에는 _____에서 여동생이 올 거예요.

    (4)   동생은 _____에 대학에 가요. 그릭고 _____을 공부할 거예요.

    (5)   동생이 _____을 좋아해요.

2. Fill in the blanks with appropriate forms of 하다 or 보다.

    (1)   여자 친구하고 자주 전화 _____

    (2)   저녁 먹고 설거지_____

    (3)   한국 마켓에서 장을 _____

    (4)   내일 심리학 시험을 _____

    (5)   스티브는 청소를 자주 안 _____

3. Change the predicates in the parentheses into the present, past, or future form based on the context.

지난 주에는 시험이 _____(많다). 그래서 아주 _____(바쁘다). 주말에는 친구들하고 같이 영화를 보러 _____(가다). 영화가 참 _____ (재미있다). 영화를 보고 중국 음식을 _____ (먹다). 다음 주말에는 여동생이 뉴욕에서 _____ (오다). 동생은 다음 학기에 대학에 가요. 그리고 심리학을 전공 _____ (하다). 동생도 저도 많이 _____ (바쁘다). 그래서 서로 전화를 자주 못 _____ (하다). 이번에 동생하고 오래간만에 이야기를 많이 _____ (하다). 동생이 한국 음식을 _____ (좋아하다). 그래서 집에서 한국 음식을 _____ (준비하다).

USAGE

A. Talking about weekend plans: 주말에 뭐 할 거예요?

[Exercise] Choose what you are going to do this weekend, and expand your narration by responding to the questions.

파티 할 거예요	무슨 파티예요? 언제예요? 누가 와요? 어디서 해요?
영화 보러 갈 거예요	무슨 영화를 볼 거예요? 누구하고 보러 갈 거예요? 영화 주인공('main character')이 누구예요?
친구를 만날 거예요	친구 이름이 뭐예요? 친구 집이 어디예요? 어디서 만나요? 친구하고 자주 만나요? 친구하고 뭐 할 거예요?
월요일에 시험이 있어요.	무슨 시험이 있어요? 몇 시간 공부할 거예요? 일요일에도 공부할 거예요? 어디서 공부할 거예요?

B. Talking about likes and dislikes

좋아해요/좋아하세요 vs. 싫어해요/싫어하세요 ('to dislike'):

리사: 유미 씨는 주말에 보통 뭐 해요?
유미: 저는 영화를 좋아해요. 그래서 영화 보러 자주 가요.
리사: 무슨 영화를 좋아해요?
유미: 코미디 영화를 좋아해요. 그리고 공포 영화도 좋아해요.
 (공포 영화 'horror movie')
 리사 씨는 공포 영화 안 좋아하세요?
리사: 네, 저는 싫어해요.

[Exercise] Talk with your partner about your favorite person, place, thing, activity, and so on, for each of the following items.

(1)	취미 'hobby'	영화 'movie', 음악 'music', 운동 'sports', 연극 'play', 독서 'reading', 여행 'travel'
(2)	영화	액션 영화 'action movie', 코미디 'comedy', 드라마 'drama', 스릴러 'thriller', 공포 영화 'horror movie'
(3)	운동	농구 'basketball', 축구 'soccer', 야구 'baseball', 풋볼 'football', 테니스 'tennis', 아이스하키 'ice hockey', 골프 'golf'
(4)	책	소설 'novel', 시 'poetry', 만화책 'comic books', 잡지 'magazine'
(5)	음식	한식 'Korean food', 일식 'Japanese food', 중식 'Chinese food', 양식 'Western food'
(6)	과목	문학 'literature', 정치학 'political science', 경제학 'economics', 심리학 'psychology', 음악 'music', 역사 'history', 생물학 'biology'

Lesson 7 The Weekend

CONVERSATION 1: I'm going to watch a movie with my friend.
(Steve and Lisa talk about their weekend plans.)

Steve:	Lisa, did you do well on your economics test yesterday?
Lisa:	Yes, I did. But it was a bit difficult. By the way, Steve, do you have any plans for this weekend?
Steve:	No, I don't.
Lisa:	I'm going to watch a movie with my friend. Why don't you join us, Steve?
Steve:	What movie are you watching?
Lisa:	An action movie.
Steve:	Okay. Then I'll go with you.
	Which movie theater do you usually go to?
Lisa:	I usually go to Broadway Theater.

CONVERSATION 2: Aren't you going to the party?

Michael:	Sophia, what are you doing next weekend?
Sophia:	I'm going to clean the house and prepare some food.
Michael:	Why?
Sophia:	My younger sister's visiting from New York.
Michael:	Then, aren't you going to the Christmas party?
Sophia:	I don't think I'll be able to make it.
Michael:	Do you see her often?
Sophia:	No, so we're going to spend a lot of time catching up.
Michael:	Okay. Then have a nice Christmas.

NARRATION: Sophia's weekend

I had a lot of exams last week; therefore, I was very busy. I went to watch a movie with some friends over the weekend. The movie was really good. After the movie we had some Chinese food. Next weekend my younger sister will be visiting from New York. She will be attending college next semester and will be majoring in psychology. My sister and I are both very busy. So we can't call each other often. For the first time in a long while, we are going to spend some time catching up. My sister really enjoys Korean food so I will make Korean food for her at home.

8과 서울에서 [In Seoul]

Conversation 1	서울 날씨가 참 좋지요?

스티브: 마크 씨, 서울 날씨가 참 좋지요?^{G8.1}

마크: 네, 아주 따뜻해요.

저는 서울의 봄 날씨를 아주 좋아해요.

스티브: 저도 그래요.

그런데 마크 씨, 이번 일요일에 시간 있어요?

마크: 네, 괜찮아요. 왜요?

스티브: 저하고 같이 광화문광장에 가요.

마크: 좋아요. 몇 시에 만나요?

스티브: 3시에 광화문광장에서 만나요.

마크: 참, 여기서^{G8.2} 광화문까지 어떻게 가요?

스티브: 162번 버스를 타고 서점 앞에서 내리세요.

광화문광장은 서점 건너편에 있어요.

마크   스티브

NEW WORDS

NOUN		PRONOUN	
가운데	the middle, the center	여기	here
건너편	the other side	거기	there
교회	church	저기	over there
꽃집	flower shop	**VERB**	
동네	neighborhood	내리다 (내리세요)	to get off
서울	Seoul	타다 (타고)	to get in/on, ride
슈퍼	supermarket	**ADJECTIVE**	
약국	drugstore	깨끗하다	to be clean
지도	map	따뜻하다 (따뜻해요)	to be warm
쪽	side, direction	조용하다	to be quiet
초등학교	elementary school	**PRE-NOUN**	
COUNTER		여러	many, several
군데	place, spot	이	③ this
번	number	그	that
SUFFIX		저	that (over there)
~지요?	isn't it? (seeking agreement)		

NEW EXPRESSIONS

1. 여기서 is a contracted form of 여기에서 (여기 'here' + 에서 'at'). The particle 에서 is often contracted to 서 as in 여기서, 거기서, 저기서, and 어디서.

2. 번 in 162번 버스 is a counter for serial numbers.

3. 광화문광장 'The Kwanghwamun Plaza'
Kwanghwamun is the main gate of Kyeongbok Palace, which was built in 1399. The municipal government launched the project with an aim to build a signature landmark for Seoul, and as a result, Kwanghwamun Plaza opened to the public on August of 2009, after 15 months of construction at a cost of about $37 million.

Exercises

1. With your partner, reconstruct conversation 1 without reading it.

리사: 소피아 씨, 오늘 _____가 참 좋지요?

소피아: 네, 참 좋아요.

리사: 이번 주말에 저하고 같이 _____에 가요.

소피아: 네, 좋아요. _____?

리사: _____에서 3시에 만나요.

소피아: 참, _____에 어떻게 가요?

리사: 145 번 버스를 _____ 교회 앞에서 _____.

그럼 건너편에 _____ 있어요.

소피아: 아, 네. 그럼 3시에 봐요.

2. Ask your classmates for directions to the following places.

A: 여기서 [서점/한국 식당/극장/백화점]까지 어떻게 가요?

B: _____

GRAMMAR

G8.1   Seeking agreement: ~지요?

Examples

(1)   A: 오늘 날씨 참 **좋지요?**   The weather is very nice
                                                    today, isn't it?
      B: 네, 정말 좋아요.   Yes, it is really nice.

(2)   A: 김 선생님, 내일 시험 **없지요?**   Professor Kim, we don't have
                                                    an exam tomorrow, do we?
      B: 네, 없어요.   No, we don't.

(3)   A: 학교 기숙사가 조용하지요?   The dorm is quiet, isn't it?
      B: 네, 조용하고 깨끗해요.   Yes, it's quiet and clean.

(4)   A: 스티브 씨, 보스톤에서 **왔지요?**   Steve, you are from
                                                    Boston, aren't you?
      B: 네, 보스톤에서 왔어요.   Yes, I am from Boston.

Note

1. ~지요? is a request for confirmation or agreement about what the speaker believes to be true. The English equivalent is 'Is that right?' or '. . . isn't it?' In contrast, ~어요/아요? is a regular question that asks for new information without any assumptions by the speaker.

Exercises

1. Fill in the blanks with ~지요 and practice with your partner.

> A: 오늘 월요일 _____ (이다)?
>
> B: 네, 월요일이에요.
>
> A: 오늘 심리학 시험이 _____ (있다)?
>
> B: 네, 있어요. 공부 많이 _____ (하다)?
>
> A: 아니요, 많이 못 했어요.

2. Translate the following expressions into Korean using ~지요?

> (1)　You don't have any question, do you?
>
> (2)　My umbrella is too small, isn't it?
>
> (3)　You don't exercise every day, do you?
>
> (4)　Professor Kim teaches Biology, doesn't he?

G8.2 Demonstrative expressions: 이/그/저

Examples

[pointing to an object]

> (1)　마크: **이** 지도 어느 서점에서 샀어요?
> 　　　유미: 학교 서점에서 샀어요.
>
> (2)　마크: (looking at two books in front)
> 　　　　　어느 책이 유미 씨 거예요?
> 　　　유미: (pointing to one of them)
> 　　　　　**이게** 제 책이에요.
> 　　　마크: (pointing to one that is on the podium)
> 　　　　　**저건** 누구 책이에요?
> 　　　유미: **저건** 스티브 거예요.
>
> (3)　마크: (pointing to a dictionary on Yumi's desk)
> 　　　　　**그** 사전 유미 씨 거예요?
> 　　　유미: 아니요, **이건** 리사 거예요. 제 거는 집에 있어요.

[pointing to a place]

(4)   A: **여기** 꽃집이 어디 있어요?   Where is the flowershop here?
       B: 여러 군데 있어요.   They are in several places.
             저기 약국 뒤에   It's behind the drugstore over there.
             꽃집이 있어요.

(5)   A: **여기** 슈퍼가 어디 있어요?   Where is the super market here?
       B: **저기** 동네 가운데에 있어요.   It's over there at the center of the
             초등학교 옆에 있어요.   town. It's next to the elementary
                                       school.

Notes

1. 이, 그, and 저 indicate the physical or mental proximity of an item relative to
the speaker and the listener.

          이   'this' (near speaker)
          그   'that' (near listener)
          저   'that over there' (away from both speaker and listener)

          이 책   그 책   저 책

2. 이, 그, and 저 are always followed by a noun.

3. 이것/그것/저것 or 이거/그거/저거: When a thing is mentioned again in the same
conversation, there is no need to repeat the noun, which can be replaced with
것/거 'thing'. 것/거 is always preceded by a modifier as in 이것, 그것, and 저것,
which correspond to 'this', 'that', and 'that over there', respectively.

    것 is often shortened to 거 in casual speech, and further contraction is made
when the following particle begins with a vowel:

Full form	Contracted form
이것/그것/저것	이거/그거/저거
이것/그것/저것 + 은 (topic particle)	이건/그건/저건
이것/그것/저것 + 이 (subject particle)	이게/그게/저게
이것/그것/저것 + 을 (object particle)	이걸/그걸/저걸

4. 여기/거기/저기: For places, 여기, 거기, or 저기 is used, where 이, 그, and 저 are built into these expressions, corresponding to 'here', 'there', and 'over there' in English, respectively.

여기, 거기, and 저기 can be used as both pronouns and adverbs of place. The locative particle 에 is often omitted, but other particles should remain.

5. Summary of demonstrative uses:

	이	그	저
thing/object	이 + N	그 + N	저 + N
person	이 사람	그 사람	저 사람
direction	이쪽 'this side'	그쪽 'that side'	저쪽 'that side over there'
place	여기 'here'	거기 'there'	저기 'over there'

Exercise

1. Practice the following dialogues with your partner, using real-life situations.

    (1)   A: [이게 / 그게 / 저게] 뭐예요?

             B: _____ 이에요/예요.

    (2)   A: [이건 / 그건 / 저건] 누구 가방이에요?

             B: _____ 가방이에요.

    (3)   A: [여기/ 거기/ 저기] 뭐가 있어요?

             B: _____있어요.

    (4)   A: [이/ 그/ 저]_____은/는 누구 거예요?

             B: _____ 거예요.

CULTURE

1. Seoul

Seoul is the capital and largest city of Korea. Situated on both sides of the Han River, Seoul, once the seat of the kings of the Chosŏn dynasty (1392–1910), is now one of the world's largest cities with over 10 million people. The Seoul

metro area, which includes the major port city of Incheon and satellite towns in 경기도, has almost 25 million residents and is the world's second-largest metropolitan area, where past and present coexist in a most fascinating manner. Almost half of the South Korean population lives in this metro area, making it the center of the economy, politics, and culture. As a global city, the city has hosted the 1988 Summer Olympics and the 2002 FIFA World Cup. The North Korean border lies about 50 km to the north. Centuries-old palaces, gates, shrines, and priceless art objects at museums attest to the illustrious past of the city, while the glistening facades of soaring skyscrapers and the bustling traffic bespeak its vibrant present.

2. Getting a taxi

As Korean taxis are very cheap, taxi drivers try to find ways to boost their earnings. Driving as fast as possible seems to be the preferred method, but picking up multiple fares is another. Even with passengers already in the car, taxi drivers might slow down for would-be passengers on the side of the road, who shout their destination to the driver. The taxi driver will pick up that fare if he or she is going in the same direction as the person already in the car. This practice is technically illegal but quite common at busy times. It offers no savings benefit for the passengers, but can increase the possibility of getting a taxi in the busy district and at busy times.

3. The subway system in Seoul

The subway is probably the most convenient means of public transportation in Seoul. Eight subway lines interlink every district of the city with every other district and with the surrounding area. The subway system carries over 8 million passengers a day. Subway stations are decorated in a combination of traditional and contemporary motifs. The ticketing and fare-collecting systems are fully automated.

Conversation 2 　말씀 좀 묻겠습니다.

마크:　　　저기요.

　　　　　말씀 좀 묻겠습니다.G8.3

　　　　　이 근처에 우체국이 어디 있습니까?

여자:　　　저기 은행 보이지요?

마크:　　　네.

여자:　　　거기서 오른쪽으로G8.4 도세요.G8.5

　　　　　그리고 쭉 가세요.

　　　　　그럼 백화점이 보일 거예요.

　　　　　우체국은 건너편에 있어요.

마크:　　　네. 감사합니다.

　　　　　참, 덕수궁은 여기서 어떻게 갑니까?

여자:　　　지하철 1호선을 타고 시청역에서 내리세요.

마크:　　　정말 감사합니다.

NEW WORDS

NOUN		VERB	
근처	nearby, vicinity	돌다 (도세요)	to turn
말씀*hon.*	speech, words (=말*plain*)	팔다	to sell
시청	city hall	묻다 (묻겠습니다)	to ask
역	station	보이다	to be seen, visible
오른쪽	right side	뵙다*hum.*	to see (=보다*plain*)
왼쪽	left side	**ADJECTIVE**	
우표	stamp	감사하다 (감사합니다)	to be thankful
은행	bank	미안하다	to be sorry
의사	doctor	**PARTICLE**	
처음	the first time	(으)로	② toward, to
호선	subway line	**SUFFIX**	
좀	a little (contraction of 조금)	~습니다/ㅂ니다	deferential ending for a statement
ADVERB		~습니까/ㅂ니까?	deferential ending for a question
쭉	straight		

NEW EXPRESSIONS

1. 저기요 (lit. 'there') is frequently used as a polite expression to gather someone's attention as in 'Excuse me'.

2. 말씀 좀 묻겠습니다 'May I ask you a question?' (lit. I will ask you something) is used as a conversation opener for asking directions as well as for seeking information. 좀, which literally means 'a little', is often used to convey politeness.

3. Directions:

이쪽	this side	오른쪽	right side
그쪽	that side	왼쪽	left side
저쪽	that side (over there)		

4. 덕수궁 is one of the four royal palaces in Seoul, built during the Chosŏn dynasty (1392~1910).

Exercise

1. Using the campus map below, ask your partner how to get to the following places.

    (1)   도서관에서 우체국까지

    (2)   운동장 ('playground')에서 기숙사까지

    (3)   서점에서 학교 식당까지

    (4)   우체국에서 서점까지

GRAMMAR

G8.3 Deferential style ~습니다/ㅂ니다, ~습니까/ㅂ니까?

Examples

(1)   A: 처음 **뵙겠습니다.**
              제 이름은 스티브 **윌슨입니다.**
    B: 저는 마크 **스미스입니다.**

(2)   A: 언제 한국에 **갑니까?**
    B: 내년 여름에 **갑니다.**

(3)   A: 지난 겨울 방학에 뭐 **했습니까?**
       B: 부모님하고 같이 여행을 **했습니다**.

Notes

1. The deferential style is used mostly in formal settings, for example, news broadcasting, conferences, business meetings, public lectures, formal interviews, and so forth. In general, male speakers tend to use the deferential style more than female speakers, who tend to use the polite ~어요/아요 style even in some formal situations. In broadcasting and conferences, however, both male and female speakers use the deferential style.

2. Even in formal conversational settings, the polite ~어요/아요 style may be used occasionally. This would make the conversation sound less formal.

   On the other hand, deferential style may be used in conversations before changing to polite style. In a first-time introduction, as in example (1), the identification of names is usually made in deferential style, particularly among male speakers. Once the communicators have introduced themselves to each other, they may begin to use the polite style. This may be attributed to the idea that before names have been given, the situation is considered formal, because no personal relationship has been established. Likewise, one may use deferential style to speak to a stranger, although many people use polite style.

3. Some fixed expressions are almost always used in deferential style.

처음 뵙겠습니다.	Nice meeting you.
실례합니다.	Excuse me.
죄송합니다/미안합니다.	I'm sorry.
감사합니다/고맙습니다	Thank you.

4. Deferential endings for statements and questions are formed as follows.

	Statement	Question
vowel-final stem	~ㅂ니다	~ㅂ니까?
consonant-final stem	~습니다	~습니까?

5. To express past events, the suffix ~습니다 / 습니까? is attached to the past suffix ~었/았/ㅆ as in the following examples.

일했어요	→	일했습니다 / 일했습니까?
배웠어요	→	배웠습니다 / 배웠습니까?

Note that [N이었습니다] is contracted to [N였습니다] when the noun ends in a vowel, as in 저희 아버지는 의사였습니다 (이 + 었 + 습니다 → 였습니다). Compare 저희 어머니는 선생님이었습니다, where no contraction occurs.

6. The following table compares deferential and polite endings for statements and questions.

Dictionary form	Speech style	Non-past		Past	
		Statement	Question	Statement	Question
먹다	Deferential	먹습니다	먹습니까?	먹었습니다	먹었습니까?
	Polite	먹어요	먹어요?	먹었어요	먹었어요?
가다	Deferential	갑니다	갑니까?	갔습니다	갔습니까?
	Polite	가요	가요?	갔어요	갔어요?
이다	Deferential	입니다	입니까?	이었습니다/였습니다	이었습니까?/였습니까?
	Polite	이에요/예요	이에요?/예요?	이었어요/였어요	이었어요?/였어요?
하다	Deferential	합니다	합니까?	했습니다	했습니까?
	Polite	해요	해요?	했어요	했어요?

Exercises

1. Change the following conversation into deferential style and practice it with your partner.

소피아: 안녕하세요? 제 이름은 소피아 왕이에요.

유미: 안녕하세요? 저는 김유미예요. 소피아 씨는 어디서 왔어요?

소피아: 저는 홍콩에서 왔어요.

유미: 학교 생활이 재미있어요? (생활 'life, living')

소피아: 네, 재미있어요. 유미 씨는 무슨 공부하세요?

유미: 심리학을 공부해요. 소피아 씨는 전공이 뭐예요?

소피아: 저는 아직 없어요. (아직 'yet')

2. Introduce yourself to your classmates in deferential style.

    (1)   Nice to meet you.

    (2)   My name is _____.

    (3)   I am _____ (nationality).

    (4)   My major is_____.

G8.4　N(으)로 'toward N'

Examples

(1)   A: 여기서 극장까지 어떻게 가요?

          B: 저기 은행 있지요?

                    거기서 오른쪽**으로** 도세요.   From there, turn right.

(2)   A: 여기 이스트 홀이 어디 있어요?

          B: 왼쪽**으로** 쭉 가세요.   Go straight to the left.

(3)   A: 오전에 어디서 만나요?

          B: 시청역 뒤**로** 오세요.

Notes

1.Two uses of (으)로 are (i) means or instrument 'by means of' (G6.1), as in 버스**로** 왔어요 'I came by bus'; and (ii) direction 'toward, to (a place)' as in the examples above.

2. (으)로 is used after a noun ending in a consonant (except /ㄹ/), and 로 after a noun ending in a vowel or the consonant /ㄹ/, as in 우체국으로, 버스로, 지하철로.

3. 에 is used to indicate a specific destination (G5.1), whereas (으)로 indicates a general direction.

        내일 서울에 갑니다.   I am going to Seoul tomorrow.

        오른쪽으로 가세요.   Go to the right.

    오른쪽에 가세요 is not acceptable because 오른쪽 is a direction, not a specific destination.

Exercise

1. Fill in the blanks with 에 or (으)로.

    (1)   여기서 오른쪽_____ 도세요.

    (2)   A: 유미 씨, 내일 뭐 할 거예요?

             B: 수영장_____ 갈 거예요.

    (3)   A: 생물학 시험이 어디서 있어요?

             B: 이스트 홀 4층_____ 가세요.

    (4)   초등학교 앞에서 왼쪽_____ 도세요.

G8.5   Irregular predicates in /ㄹ/

Examples

(1)   A: 한국 역사를 잘 **압니까?**   Do you know Korean history?
         B: 네, 좀 알아요.   Yes, I know some.

(2)   A: 어디 **사세요?**   Where do you live?
         B: 서울에서 살아요.   I live in Seoul.

(3)   A: 은행이 여기서 **멉니까?**   Is the bank far from here?
         B: 네, 좀 멀어요.   Yes, it is rather far.

Notes

1. When an adjective or verb stem ending in /ㄹ/ is followed by /ㄴ/, /ㅂ/, or /ㅅ/, the final /ㄹ/ is omitted. In case of the honorific ending ~으세요, the vowel 으 is deleted. Then, the stem-final /ㄹ/ is omitted before /ㅅ/: 살 + 으세요 → 살 + 세요 → 사세요.

	~ㅂ니다	~(으)세요	~어/아요	~었/았어요	~(으)ㄹ 거예요
돌다 'to turn'	돕니다	도세요	돌아요	돌았어요	돌 거예요
살다 'to live'	삽니다	사세요	살아요	살았어요	살 거예요
만들다 'to make'	만듭니다	만드세요	만들어요	만들었어요	만들 거예요

Exercises

1. Change the polite style into the deferential style.

     (1)   저는 교회 근처에 살아요.   → <u>저는 교회 근처에 삽니다.</u>

     (2)   도서관에서 우체국까지 멀어요. → _____

     (3)   학교 서점에서 지도를 팔아요. → _____

     (4)   저는 그 사람을 잘 알아요.   → _____

2. Answer the following questions using the deferential style.

     (1)   동생은 어디서 살아요?

              <u>로스앤젤레스에서 삽니다.</u>

     (2)   지금 어디서 사세요?   (3)   김 선생님을 아세요?

              _____   _____

     (4)   집이 학교에서 멀어요?   (5)   어디서 우표를 팔아요?

                                   _____

4 min

| Narration | 우리 동네 |

안녕하세요? 제 이름은 스티브 월슨입니다. 저는 미국
보스톤에서 왔습니다. 지금은 서울에서 한국어를 배웁니다.
저는 학교 근처 아파트에서 삽니다. 아파트가 조용하고
깨끗합니다.
이게 우리 동네 지도입니다. 동네 가운데 초등학교가 있습니다.
학교 뒤에는 교회가 있습니다. 교회 옆에는 백화점이 있습니다.
백화점 왼쪽에는 꽃집이 있습니다. 꽃집 옆에는 서점이 있고
서점 옆에는 식당이 있습니다. 극장은 약국 건너편에 있고
우체국은 슈퍼 옆에 있습니다. 그리고 커피숍이 여러 군데
있습니다.

Exercises

1. Read the narration and answer the following questions.

      (1)   스티브는 지금 어디서 삽니까?

      (2)   스티브 아파트는 어디 있습니까?

      (3)   교회는 어디 있습니까?

      (4)   백화점은 어디 있습니까?

      (5)   서점은 어디 있습니까?

      (6)   약국은 어디 있습니까?

      (7)   꽃집 오른쪽에 뭐가 있습니까?

2. Change the polite ending in the parentheses into the deferential ending.

안녕하세요? 제 이름은 스티브 윌슨_____(이에요). 저는 미국
보스톤에서_____ (왔어요). 지금은 서울에서 한국어를 _____
(배워요). 저는 학교 근처 아파트에서_____ (살아요). 아파트가
조용하고_____ (깨끗해요). 이게 우리 동네 지도_____
(예요). 동네 가운데 초등학교가_____ (있어요). 학교 뒤에는
교회가_____ (있어요). 교회 옆에는 백화점이 있습니다.

3. Based on the reading, fill in the blanks with the appropriate words provided below.

군데	에서	이게	가운데	꽃집
뒤	왼쪽	약국	근처	

안녕하세요? 제 이름은 스티브 윌슨입니다. 저는 미국 보스톤_____ 왔습니다.
지금은 서울에서 한국어를 배웁니다. 저는 학교 _____ 아파트에서 삽니다.
아파트가 조용하고 깨끗합니다. _____ 우리 동네 지도입니다. 동네 _____
초등학교가 있습니다. 학교 _____에는 교회가 있습니다. 교회 옆에는 백화점이
있습니다. 백화점 _____에는 꽃집이 있습니다. _____ 옆에는 서점이 있고
서점 옆에는 식당이 있습니다. 극장은 _____ 건너편에 있고 우체국은 슈퍼
옆에 있습니다. 그리고 커피숍이 여러 _____ 있습니다.

USAGE

A. Conversing and inquiring about someone's background

When you want to know about someone's background (for example, the town or country s/he comes from), the question 어디서 오셨어요? 'Where are you from?' is often used (어디서 is a contracted form of 어디에서). The response to this question is [place/location]에서 왔어요, as shown in the following example.

스티브:	저는 미국에서 왔어요.
	마크 씨는 어디서 오셨어요?
마크:	저는 호주 시드니에서 왔어요.
	(호주 'Australia' ; 시드니 'Sydney')

When you specify a town or a city you came from along with the country, the larger unit (country) should precede the smaller (city): 호주 시드니에서 instead of 시드니 호주에서.

고향이 어디예요? 'Where is your hometown?' can be used instead of 어디서 오셨어요?

A:	고향이 어디예요?
B:	서울이에요.

Note that 어디예요? and 어디 있어요? are sometimes interchangeable. However, in the case of 고향 'hometown', 고향이 어디 있어요? is unacceptable. In general, movable objects such as 책 are not used with the copula 이다, but they are used with the existential predicate 있다.

고향이 어디예요?	[O]	고향이 어디 있어요?	[X]
책이 어디 있어요?	[O]	책이 어디예요?	[X]

[Exercise 1] Practice the following dialogue with your classmate.

스티브:	안녕하세요? 제 이름은 스티브 윌슨입니다.
마크:	네, 안녕하세요? 저는 마크 스미스입니다.
스티브:	마크 씨는 어디서 오셨어요?
마크:	호주 시드니에서 왔어요. 스티브 씨는 고향이 어디예요?
스티브:	제 고향은 보스톤이에요.

마크:　　　　　서울에 언제 오셨어요?

스티브:　　　　8월 24일에 왔어요.

Now exchange the following information.

A:　　　안녕하세요? 제 이름은 _____

B:　　　네, 안녕하세요? 저는 _____

　　　　　　　　　　_____에서 왔어요.

　　　　　　　　_____ 씨는 어디서 오셨어요?

A:　　　저는 _____에서 왔어요.

B:　　　_____ (the place you live in now)에 언제 오셨어요?

A:　　　_____년 (year) 에 왔어요.

Practice the conversation again, using deferential style.

[Exercise 2] Let's find out where each student in the chart below came from. Play different roles according to the sample dialogue.

Student	Country	State/town
스티브	미국	보스톤
소피아	중국	홍콩
미치코	일본	도쿄
마크	호주	시드니

스티브:　　　소피아 씨, 어디서 왔어요?

소피아:　　　중국에서 왔어요.

스티브:　　　아, 그래요? 중국 어디서 왔어요?

소피아:　　　홍콩에서 왔어요.

B. Asking and giving directions

When you want to ask for directions on the street in Korea, it is best to start with
실례합니다 'Excuse me', a polite way to seek someone's attention. People will
expect this expression to be followed by a question about directions.

(1)   A: 저어, 실례합니다.
              말씀 좀 묻겠습니다.
       B: 네.
       A: 이 근처에 우체국이 어디 있어요?
       B: 저기 은행 옆에 있어요.

(Note: 저어 is used at the beginning of
conversation to get the other person's attention,
and also for hesitation.)

For more specific directions, you may ask 어떻게 가요? For instance:

(2)   A: 여기서 어떻게 가요?   How do I go from here?
       B: 쭉 가세요.   Go straight.
              그럼 오른쪽에 있어요.   Then it is on your right side.
       A: 감사합니다.

(으)로 가세요 'go toward the direction of . . .' is often used to give directions. More
expressions asking about directions follow.

오른쪽으로 도세요.	Turn right.
왼쪽으로 도세요.	Turn left.
똑바로 가세요.	Go straight.
길을 건너세요.	Cross the street.
사거리에서 오른쪽으로 가세요.	Go right at the intersection.
신호등에서 왼쪽으로 도세요.	Turn left at the traffic light.
극장은 약국 건너편에 있어요.	The theater is across from the drugstore.

[Exercise 1] Ask and give directions for each location on the basis of dialogues (1) and (2) above.

(1)   은행
(2)   우체국
(3)   극장
(4)   약국
(5)   커피숍

Lesson 8 In Seoul

CONVERSATION 1: The weather in Seoul is beautiful, isn't it?

Steve:	Mark, the weather in Seoul is beautiful, isn't it?
Mark:	Yes, it's very warm. I really like spring in Seoul.
Steve:	Me too. It's very warm in spring. By the way, do you have some time this Sunday?
Mark:	Yes, I do. Why?
Steve:	Let's go to the Kwanghwamun Plaza.
Mark:	Sounds good. Where shall we meet?
Steve:	At the plaza at three o'clock.
Mark:	By the way, how do I get to the plaza from here?
Steve:	Take bus number 162 and get off in front of the bookstore. The plaza is across from the bookstore.

CONVERSATION 2: May I ask you something?

Mark:	Excuse me. May I ask you something? Is there a post office nearby?
Woman:	Do you see the bank over there?
Mark:	Yes.
Woman:	Turn right from there, and go straight ahead. Then you'll see the department store. The post office is across from the department store.
Mark:	Okay, I see. Thank you. By the way, how do I get to the Tŏksu Palace?
Woman:	Take subway line 1 and then get off at the City Hall Station.
Mark:	Thank you so much.

NARRATION: Our Neighborhood

Hello. My name is Steve Wilson. I'm from Boston, United States. I'm currently learning Korean in Seoul. I live at the apartment near school. The apartment is quiet and clean. This is a map of our neighborhood. There is an elementary school in the middle of the neighborhood. There is a church behind the school. There is a department store next to the church. On the left side of the department store is a flower shop. Next to the flower shop is a bookstore, and next to the bookstore is a restaurant. The theater is across from the drugstore, and the post office is next to the supermarket. Also, there are coffee shops in several places.

Appendices

Appendix 1-1. Copula, Adjective, and Verb Conjugations

Grammar	Dictionary form / Patterns	이다	아니다	있다	계시다	되다	하다 Adjective: 깨끗하다 / Verb: 공부하다
G7.3	~고 clausal connective	(이)고	아니고	있고	계시고	되고	깨끗하고 / 공부하고
G7.1	~(으)ㄹ 거예요 probability	(이)ㄹ 거예요	아닐 거예요	있을 거예요	계실 거예요	될 거예요	깨끗할 거예요 / 공부할 거예요
G5.3	~(으)러 purpose	-	-	-	-	-	- / 공부하러
G3.2	~(으)세요 honorific polite	(이)세요	아니세요	있으세요	-	되세요	깨끗하세요 / 공부하세요
G8.3	~습니다/ㅂ니다 ~습니까/ㅂ니까? deferential	입니다 입니까?	아닙니다 아닙니까?	있습니다 있습니까?	계십니다 계십니까?	됩니다 됩니까?	깨끗합니다 깨끗합니까? / 합니다 합니까?
G2.5	~어요/아요 polite	이에요/ 예요	아니에요	있어요	계세요	되어요 돼요	깨끗해요 / 공부해요
G8.3	~었/았습니다 past deferential	이었습니다/ 였습니다	아니었습니다	있었습니다	계셨습니다	되었습니다	깨끗했습니다 / 공부했습니다
G6.3	~었/았어요 past	이었어요/ 였어요	아니었어요	있었어요	계셨어요	되었어요	깨끗했어요 / 공부했어요
G8.1	~지요? seeking agreement	(이)지요?	아니지요?	있지요?	계시지요?	되지요?	깨끗하지요? / 공부하지요?

Appendix 1-2. Conjugation of Irregular Adjectives and Verbs

Lesson	Dictionary form / Patterns	-ㄷ 듣다 걷다 묻다	-ㄹ ADJ: 멀다 길다 / V: 팔다, 놀다, 돌다, 만들다, 살다, 알다	-ㅂ ADJ: : 춥다, 덥다 쉽다, 어렵다 반갑다, 즐겁다 / V: 돕다
G7.3	~고 clausal connective	듣고	멀고 / 열고	춥고 / 돕고
G7.1	~(으)ㄹ 거예요 probability	들을 거예요	멀 거예요 길 거예요 / 열 거예요	추울 거예요 / 도울 거예요
G5.3	~(으)러 purpose	들으러	- / 열러	- / 도우러
G3.2	~(으)세요 honorific polite	들으세요	머세요 / 여세요	추우세요 / 도우세요
G8.3	~습니다/ㅂ니다 ~습니까?/ㅂ니까? deferential	듣습니다 듣습니까?	멉니다 / 엽니까?	춥습니다 / 돕습니까?
G2.5	~어요/아요 polite	들어요	멀어요 / 열어요	추워요 / 도와요
G8.3	~었/았습니다 deferential (past)	들었습니다	멀었습니다 / 열었습니다	추웠습니다 / 도왔습니다
G6.3	~었/았어요 past/completed	들었어요	멀었어요 / 열었어요	추웠어요 / 도왔어요
G8.1	~지요? seeking agreement	듣지요?	멀지요? / 열지요?	춥지요? / 돕지요?

Lesson	Patterns / Dictionary form	– 으 ADJ: 크다 바쁘다 V: 쓰다	– 르 ADJ: 다르다 빠르다 V:부르다 모르다
G7.3	~고 clausal connective	크고 바쁘고 쓰고	다르고 부르고
G7.1	~(으)ㄹ 거예요 probability	클 거예요 바쁠 거예요 쓸 거예요	다를 거예요 부를 거예요
G5.3	~(으)러 purpose	- 쓰러	- 부르러
G3.2	~(으)세요 honorific polite	크세요 바쁘세요 쓰세요	다르세요 부르세요
G8.3	~습니다/ㅂ니다 ~습니까?/ㅂ니까? deferential	큽니다 바쁩니다 씁니다	다릅니다 부릅니다
G2.5	~어요/아요 polite	커요 바빠요 써요	달라요 불러요
G8.3	~었/았습니다 deferential (past)	컸습니다 바빴습니다 썼습니다	달랐습니다 불렀습니다
G6.3	~었/았어요 past/completed	컸어요 바빴어요 썼어요	달랐어요 불렀어요
G8.1	~지요? seeking agreement	크지요? 바쁘지요? 쓰지요?	다르지요? 부르지요?

Appendix 1-3. The Three Types of Conjugation

Conjugations for adjectives and verbs can be classified into the following three types:

    A. stem + 어/아
    B. stem + (으)
    C. no change in stem

A. Stem + 어/아	B. Stem + (으)	C. No change in stem
~어요/아요 ~었/았/ㅆ	~(으)ㄹ 거예요 ~(으)러 ~(으)세요	~고 ~지요

Appendix 2. Kinship Terms

1. 가족 'family'; 식구 'member of a family'

부모	parents		딸	daughter (plain)
부모님	parents (hon.)		따님	daughter (hon.)
아버지	father		맏딸	first daughter
아버님	father (hon.)		외딸	only daughter
어머니	mother		형제	sibling(s)
어머님	mother (hon.)		형	male's older brother
할아버지	grandfather		형님	male's older brother (hon.)
할머니	grandmother		누나	male's older sister
남편	husband		누님	male's older sister (honorific)
아내	wife (plain)		오빠	female's older brother
부인	wife (hon.)		언니	female's older sister
아들	son (plain)		남동생	younger brother
아드님	son (hon.)		여동생	younger sister
맏아들	first son		막내	youngest child
외아들	only son			

2. 친척 'relative(s)'

아저씨	uncle
아주머니	aunt
큰아버지	uncle (who is one's father's older brother)
큰어머니	aunt (who is the wife of one's father's older brother)
작은아버지	uncle (who is one's father's younger brother)
작은어머니	aunt (who is the wife of one's father's younger brother)
삼촌	uncle (who is one's father's younger brother)
숙모	aunt (who is the wife of one's father's younger brother)
외삼촌	uncle (who is one's mother's brother)
외숙모	aunt (who is the wife of one's mother's brother)
고모	aunt (who is one's father's sister)
이모	aunt (who is one's mother's sister)
사촌	cousin

Appendix 3. Numbers

Arabic numeral	Sino-Korean	Native Korean	Native Korean before counters
0	영 or 공	-	-
1	일	하나	한
2	이	둘	두
3	삼	셋	세
4	사	넷	네
5	오	다섯	다섯
6	육	여섯	여섯
7	칠	일곱	일곱
8	팔	여덟	여덟
9	구	아홉	아홉
10	십	열	열
11	십일	열하나	열한
12	십이	열둘	열두
13	십삼	열셋	열세
14	십사	열넷	열네
15	십오	열다섯	열다섯
16	십육 [심늌]	열여섯	열여섯
17	십칠	열일곱	열일곱
18	십팔	열여덟	열여덟
19	십구	열아홉	열아홉
20	이십	스물	스무
30	삼십	서른	서른
40	사십	마흔	마흔
50	오십	쉰	쉰
60	육십	예순	예순
70	칠십	일흔	일흔
80	팔십	여든	여든
90	구십	아흔	아흔
100	백		
1,000	천		
10,000	만		

Large Numbers

100	백	200	이백
1,000	천	2,000	이천
10,000	만	20,000	이만
100,000	십만	200,000	이십만
1,000,000	백만	2,000,000	이백만
10,000,000	천만	20,000,000	이천만
100,000,000	억	200,000,000	이억
1,000,000,000	십억	2,000,000,000	이십억
10,000,000,000	백억	20,000,000,000	이백억
100,000,000,000	천억	200,000,000,000	이천억
1,000,000,000,000	조	2,000,000,000,000	이조

Appendix 4. Counters

A. With Sino-Korean numbers

Counters	층	분	과	년	월	일
What is being counted	Floors of a building	Minutes	Lesson (in order)	Years	Months	Days
1	일 층	일 분	일 과	일 년	일월	일 일
2	이 층	이 분	이 과	이 년	이월	이 일
3	삼 층	삼 분	삼 과	삼 년	삼월	삼 일
4	사 층	사 분	사 과	사 년	사월	사 일
5	오 층	오 분	오 과	오 년	오월	오 일
6	육 층	육 분	육 과	육 년	유월	육 일
10	십 층	십 분	십 과	십 년	시월	십 일
12	십이 층	십이 분	십이 과	십이 년	십이월	십이 일

Counters	달러(불)	원	마일	학년	번	주일
What is being counted	Dollars	Won (Korean currency)	Mile	School years	Numbers (serial)	Weeks
1	일 달러	일 원	일 마일	일학년	일 번	일 주일
2	이 달러	이 원	이 마일	이학년	이 번	이 주일
3	삼 달러	삼 원	삼 마일	삼학년	삼 번	삼 주일
4	사 달러	사 원	사 마일	사학년	사 번	사 주일
5	오 달러	오 원	오 마일	오학년	오 번	오 주일
6	육 달러	육 원	육 마일	육학년	육 번	육 주일
10	십 달러	십 원	십 마일	십학년	십 번	십 주일
12	십이 달러	십이 원	십이 마일	십이학년	십이 번	십이 주일

B. With Native Korean numbers

Counters	명/사람	분	시	시간	달	마리	살	과목
What is being counted	People	People (honorific)	Point of time: 'the hour'	Duration: 'hours'	Duration: 'months'	Animals	Age: 'years old'	Academic subjects
1	한 명 한 사람	한 분	한 시	한 시간	한 달	한 마리	한 살	한 과목
2	두 명 두 사람	두 분	두 시	두 시간	두 달	두 마리	두 살	두 과목
3	세 명 세 사람	세 분	세 시	세 시간	세 달	세 마리	세 살	세 과목
4	네 명 네 사람	네 분	네 시	네 시간	네 달	네 마리	네 살	네 과목
5	다섯 명 다섯 사람	다섯 분	다섯 시	다섯 시간	다섯 달	다섯 마리	다섯 살	다섯 과목
6	여섯 명 여섯 사람	여섯 분	여섯 시	여섯 시간 열 시간	여섯 달	여섯 마리	여섯 살	여섯 과목
10	열 명 열 사람	열 분	열 시		열 달	열 마리	열 살	열 과목

Counters	과	개	권	장	병	잔	번	대
What is being counted	Number of lessons	Items	Volumes	Sheets (of paper)	Bottles	Cups and glasses	Times	Vehicles, cars
1	한 과	한 개	한 권	한 장	한 병	한 잔	한 번	한 대
2	두 과	두 개	두 권	두 장	두 병	두 잔	두 번	두 대
3	세 과	세 개	세 권	세 장	세 병	세 잔	세 번	세 대
4	네 과	네 개	네 권	네 장	네 병	네 잔	네 번	네 대
5	다섯 과	다섯 개	다섯 권	다섯 장	다섯 병	다섯 잔	다섯 번	다섯 대
6	여섯 과	여섯 개	여섯 권	여섯 장	여섯 병	여섯 잔	여섯 번	여섯 대
10	열 과	열 과	열 권	열 장	열 병	열 잔	열 번	열 대

Grammar Index

L = lesson, C = conversation, G = grammar

Item	Meaning	Lesson	
(으)로	'by means of'	L6C1	G6.1
(으)로	'toward, to'	L8C2	G8.4
~(으)ㄹ 거예요	probability suffix	L7C1	G7.1
~(으)러	'in order to'	L5C2	G5.3
~(으)세요	honorific polite ending	L3C1	G3.2
~고	'and' (clausal connective)	L7C2	G7.3
~습니다/ㅂ니다	deferential ending for a statement	L8C2	G8.3
~습니까/ㅂ니까	deferential ending for a question	L8C2	G8.3
~어요/아요	polite ending	L2C2	G2.5
~었/았/ㅆ	past tense	L6C2	G6.3
~지요	'. . . isn't it?' (seeking agreement)	L8C1	G8.1
그	demonstrative expression: 'that'	L8C1	G8.2
도	comparing items: 'also, too'	L1C1	G1.3
못	negative adverb: 'cannot'	L6C2	G6.4
무슨	'what (kind of) N'	L7C1	G7.2
아니에요	'to not be' (identification)	L1C2	G1.5
안	negative adverb: 'do not'	L6C2	G6.4
어느	'which N'	L7C1	G7.2
에	'in, at, on' (indicates a static location)	L2C1	G2.2
에	'to' (destination)	L5C1	G5.1
에	'at' (time)	L5C2	
에서	'in, at' (dynamic location)	L5C1	G5.1
은/는	topic particle: 'as for'	L1C1	G1.1
	comparing items	L1C1	G1.3
	changing topics	L2C1	G2.3
을/를	object particle	L3C2	G3.3
이	demonstrative expression: 'this'	L8C1	G8.2
이/가	subject particle	L2C1	G2.1
이에요/예요	'to be' (equation)	L1C1	G1.1
저	demonstrative: 'that (over there)'	L8C1	G8.2

Korean - English Glossary

1학년	freshman	구두 시험	oral exam
2학년	sophomore	군데	place, spot
3학년	junior	권	volume (counter)
4학년	senior	그	that
6월	June (유월)	그래서	so, therefore
가	subject particle	그런데	1. but, however;
가게	store		2. by the way
가깝다	to be close, near	그럼	(if so) then
가끔	sometimes	그렇다	to be so
가다	to go	그리고	and
가르치다	to teach	극장	movie theater
가방	bag	근처	nearby, vicinity
가운데	the middle, the center	금요일	Friday
가을	autumn, fall	기계 공학	mechanical engineering
감사하다	to be thankful	기숙사	dormitory
같이	together	길	street, road
개¹	dog	까지	up to (location)
개²	item (counter)	깨끗하다	to be clean
거	thing (contraction of 것)	꽃	flower
		꽃집	flower shop
거기	there	끝나다	to end
건너편	the other side	나 *plain*	I (=저 *hum.*)
건축학	architecture	나라	country
걷다	to walk	나쁘다	to be bad
걸리다	to take [time]	나오다	to come out
것	thing (=거)	날마다	every day
겨울	winter	날씨	weather
경제학	economics	남동생	younger brother
계시다 *hon.*	to be (existence), stay	남자	man
계절	season	내 *plain*	my (=제 *hum.*)
고등학교	high school	내년	next year
고등학생	high school student	내리다	to get off
고맙다	to be thankful	내일	tomorrow
고향	hometown	너	you
골프	golf	너무	too much
공	0 (zero: for phone #)	넓다	to be spacious, wide
공부	study	네	1. yes; 2. I see; 3. okay
공부하다	to study	년	year (counter)
공원	park	농구	basketball
공포 영화	horror movie	누가	who (누구+가)
과	lesson, chapter	누구	who
과목	course, subject	누나	the older sister of a
괜찮다	to be all right, okay		male
교과서	textbook	뉴스	news
교실	classroom	뉴욕	New York
교육학	education	는	topic particle ('as for')
교회	church	다시	again

다음	next, following	말하다	to speak
달	month (counter)	맛없다	to be tasteless, not
달러	dollar (=불)		delicious
대통령	president	맛있다	to be delicious
대학	college, university	매년	every year
대학교	college, university	매달	every month
대학생	college student	매일	every day
대학원	graduate school	매주	every week
대학원생	graduate student	먹다	to eat
덥다	to be hot	멀다	to be far
덮다	to close, cover	멕시코	Mexico
도	also, too	명	people (counter)
도서관	library	몇	how many, what
도쿄	Tokyo	모르다	to not know
독서	reading	목요일	Thursday
돈	money	못	cannot
돌	the first birthday	무슨	what, what kind of
돌다	to turn	무엇	what (=뭐)
동네	neighborhood	문학	literature
동생	younger sibling	묻다	to ask
동양학	Asian Studies	물리학	physics
두	two (with counter)	뭐	what (=무엇)
둘	two	미국	the United States
뒤	the back, behind	미안하다	to be sorry
드라마	drama	밑	the bottom, below
듣다	1. to listen;	바쁘다	to be busy
	2. to take a course	밖	outside
들	plural particle	반¹	class
따뜻하다	to be warm	반²	half
따라하다	to repeat after	반갑다	to be glad
똑바로	straight, upright	받다	to receive
뛰다	to run	밤	night
랩	lab	방	room
러시아	Russia	방학	school vacation
로스앤젤레스	Los Angeles (L.A.)	배우다	to learn
룸메이트	roommate	백화점	department store
를	object particle	버스	bus
마리	animal (counter)	번	number (counter)
마시다	to drink	번호	number
마켓	market	법학	law
만	only	보내다	to spend time;
만나다	to meet	보다	to see, look, watch
만들다	to make	보스톤	Boston
만화책	comic book	보이다	to be seen, visible
많다	to be many, much	보통	usually
많이	much, many	볼펜	ballpoint pen
말	speech, words	봄	spring
말씀 *hon.*	speech, words (=말	뵙다 *hum.*	to see (=보다 *plain*)
	plain)	부모님	parents

부자	a wealthy person
분	minute (counter)
불	dollar (=달러)
브로드웨이 극장	Broadway theater
비싸다	to be expensive
비행기	airplane
빌딩	building
사	4
사거리	intersection
사다	to buy
사람	person, people
사이	1. relationship;
	2. between
사전	dictionary
사진	photo, picture
살다	to live
삼	3
새벽	dawn
생물학	biology
생일	birthday
생활	life, living
서로	each other
서울	Seoul
서점	bookstore (=책방)
선물	present, gift
선물하다	to give a present, gift
선생님	teacher
설거지	dishwashing
설거지하다	to wash dishes
성함 *hon.*	name (=이름 *plain*)
센트	cent
소설	novel
쇼핑	shopping
쇼핑하다	to shop
수도	capital (city)
수업	course, class
수영	swimming
수영장	swimming pool
수영하다	to swim
수요일	Wednesday
숙제	homework
숙제하다	to do homework
쉽다	to be easy
슈퍼	supermarket
스릴러	thriller
스페인	Spain
시[1]	hour, o'clock
시[2]	poetry
시간	time, hour (duration)
시계	clock, watch
시드니	Sydney
시청	city hall
시청역	city hall station
시카고	Chicago
시험	test, exam
식당	restaurant
신문	newspaper
신호등	traffic light
싫어하다	to dislike
심리학	psychology
싸다	to be cheap
쓰다	to write
씨	attached to a person's name for courtesy
아	oh
아니다	to not be (negative equation)
아니요	no
아마	probably, perhaps
아버지	father
아이스하키	ice hockey
아주	very, really
아직	yet, still
아침	1. breakfast;
	2. morning
아파트	apartment
안[1]	the inside
안[2]	do not
안녕하다	to be well
안녕히	in peace
앉다	to sit
알다	to know
앞	the front
액션	action
야구	baseball
약국	drugstore
약속	1. engagement;
	2. promise
양식	Western style (food)
애기	talk, chat (=이야기)
애기하다	to talk, chat
어	oh
어느	which
어디	what place, where
어떻게	how
어떻다	to be how
어렵다	to be difficult
어머니	mother

어제	yesterday	왜	why
언니	the older sister of a female	왼쪽	left side
		요즘	these days
언어학	linguistics	우리 *plain*	we/us/our (=저희 *hum.*)
언제	when	우산	umbrella
얼마	how long/much	우체국	post office
얼마나	how long/much	우표	stamp
없다	1. to not be (existence); 2. to not have	운동	exercise
		운동장	playground
에	1. in, at, on (indicates a static location)	운동하다	to exercise
		운전하다	to drive
		원	won (Korean currency)
	2. to (destination)	월	month (counter)
	3. at, in, on (time)	월요일	Monday
에서	1. in, at (dynamic location)	위	the top side, above
		유니온 빌딩	Union Building
	2. from (location)	으로¹	by means of
여기	here	으로²	toward, to
여동생	younger sister	은	topic particle ('as for')
여러	many, several	은행	bank
여름	summer	을	object particle
여자	woman	음식	food
여자 친구	girlfriend	음악	music
여행	travel	의	of
여행하다	to travel	의사	doctor
역	station	의자	chair
역사	history	이¹	2
연극	play	이²	subject particle
연습	practice	이³	this
연습하다	to practice	이거	this (=이것)
연필	pencil	이다	to be (equation)
열심히	diligently	이름	name
영	0 (zero)	이메일	e-mail
영국	the United Kingdom	이번	this time
영어	the English language	이스트 홀	East Hall
영화	movie	이야기	talk, chat (=얘기)
옆	the side, beside	이야기하다	to talk (=얘기하다)
예	yes, I see, okay (=네)	인구	population
예쁘다	to be pretty	인사	greeting
오늘	today	인사하다	to greet
오다	to come	일¹	1
오래간만	after a long time	일²	day (counter)
오른쪽	right side	일³	work
오빠	the older brother of a female	일본	Japan
		일식	Japanese style (food)
오전	a.m.	일어나다	to get up
오후	afternoon	일요일	Sunday
올해	this year	일하다	to work
옷	clothes	읽다	to read

있다	1. to be (existence); 2. to have	중학생	middle school student
자다	to sleep	지금	now
자전거	bicycle	지난	last, past
자주	often, frequently	지내다	to get along
작년	last year	지도	map
작다	to be small (in size)	지하철	subway
잘	well	질문	question
잡지	magazine	집	home, house
장(을) 보다	to buy one's groceries	짧다	to be short
재미없다	to be uninteresting	쪽	side, direction
재미있다	to be interesting, fun	쭉	straight
저	that (over there)	쯤	about, around
저 *hum.*	I (=나 *plain*)	차	car
저기	over there	참	1. really, truly; 2. by the way
저녁	1. evening; 2. dinner	책	book
저어	uh (expression of hesitation)	책방	bookstore
		책상	desk
		처음	the first time
저희 *hum.*	we/us/our (=우리 *plain*)	천천히	slow(ly)
전공	major	청소	cleaning
전공하다	to major	청소하다	to clean
전기공학	electrical engineering	초등학교	elementary school
전화	telephone	초등학생	elementary school student
전화 번호	telephone number		
전화하다	to make a telephone call	축구	soccer
		축하하다	to congratulate
점심	lunch	춥다	to be cold
정말	really	취미	hobby
정치학	political science	층	floor, layer (counter)
제 *hum.*	my (=내 *plain*)	치다	to play (tennis)
조금	a little (= 좀)	친구	friend
조용하다	to be quiet	칠판	blackboard
좀	a little (contraction of 조금)	캐나다	Canada
		캠퍼스	campus
좁다	to be narrow	커피	coffee
좋다	to be good, nice	커피숍	coffee shop, cafe
좋아하다	to like	컴퓨터	computer
죄송하다	to be sorry	컴퓨터 랩	computer lab
주	week	코미디	comedy
주다	to give	쿠바	Cuba
주말	weekend	크게	loud(ly)
주스	juice	크다	to be big
주인공	main character	크리스마스	Christmas
준비	preparation	클래스	class
준비하다	to prepare	클래식	classic
중국	China	타다	to get in/on, ride
중식	Chinese style (food)	테니스	tennis
중학교	middle school	테니스장	tennis court

텔레비전	television	학년	school year
토요일	Saturday	학생	student
트럭	truck	학생회관	student center
파티	party	한	one (with counter)
팔다	to sell	한국	Korea
펜	pen	한국말	the Korean language
펴다	to open, unfold	한국어	the Korean language
풋볼	football	한식	Korean style (food)
프랑스	France	한인타운	Korea town
하고	1. and (with nouns); 2. with	햄버거	hamburger
하나	one	형	the older brother of a male
하다	to do	호선	subway line
하루	(one) day	호주	Australia
하와이	Hawai'i	홍콩	Hong Kong
학교	school	화요일	Tuesday
학기	semester, academic term	흐리다	to be cloudy

English - Korean Glossary

0 (zero)	영	Boston	보스톤
0 (zero)	공 (for phone #)	bottom, below	밑
1	일	breakfast	아침
2	이	Broadway theater	브로드웨이 극장
3	삼	building	빌딩
4	사	bus	버스
a.m.	오전	busy	바쁘다
about, around	쯤	but, however	그런데
action	액션	buy	사다
afternoon	오후	buy one's groceries	장(을) 보다
again	다시	by means of	(으)로
airplane	비행기	by the way	그런데
also, too	도	by the way	참
and	그리고	Canada	캐나다
and (with nouns)	하고	cafe	커피숍
animal	마리 (counter)	campus	캠퍼스
apartment	아파트	cannot	못
architecture	건축학	capital (city)	수도
Asian studies	동양학	car	차
ask	묻다	cent	센트
at, in, on (time)	에	chair	의자
attached to a person's name	씨	cheap	싸다
Australia	호주	Chicago	시카고
autumn, fall	가을	China	중국
back, behind	뒤	Chinese style (food)	중식
bad	나쁘다	Christmas	크리스마스
bag	가방	church	교회
ballpoint pen	볼펜	city hall	시청
bank	은행	city hall station	시청역
baseball	야구	class	반
basketball	농구	class	클래스
be (existence)	계시다 *hon.*	classic	클래식
be (existence)	있다 *plain*	classroom	교실
be (for identification)	이다	clean	깨끗하다
be all right, okay	괜찮다	clean	청소하다
be seen, visible	보이다	cleaning	청소
be small (in size)	작다	clock, watch	시계
between	사이	close, cover	덮다
bicycle	자전거	close, near	가깝다
big	크다	clothes	옷
biology	생물학	cloudy	흐리다
birthday	생일	coffee	커피
blackboard	칠판	coffee shop	커피숍
book	책	cold	춥다
bookstore	서점	college	대학교
bookstore	책방	college student	대학생
		come	오다

comedy	코미디	every day	매일
come out	나오다	every month	매달
comic book	만화책	every week	매주
computer	컴퓨터	every year	매년
computer lab	컴퓨터 랩	exercise	운동
congratulate	축하하다	exercise	운동하다
country	나라	expensive	비싸다
course, class	수업	far	멀다
course, subject	과목	father	아버지
Cuba	쿠바	first birthday	돌
dawn	새벽	first time	처음
day	일	first time in a while	오래간만
day	하루(one day)	floor, layer	층 (1층, 2층)
delicious	맛있다	flower	꽃
department store	백화점	flower shop	꽃집
desk	책상	food	음식
dictionary	사전	football	풋볼
difficult	어렵다	France	프랑스
diligently	열심히	freshman	1학년
dinner	저녁	Friday	금요일
dish wash	설거지하다	friend	친구
dishwashing	설거지	from	에서 (location)
dislike	싫어하다	front	앞
do	하다	get along	지내다
doctor	의사	get in/on, ride	타다
dog	개	get off	내리다
dollar	불, 달러	get up	일어나다
do not	안	girlfriend	여자 친구
dormitory	기숙사	give	주다
drama	드라마	give a present, gift	선물하다
drink	마시다	glad	반갑다
drive	운전하다	go	가다
drugstore	약국	golf	골프
each other	서로	good, nice	좋다
East Hall	이스트 홀	graduate school	대학원
easy	쉽다	graduate student	대학원생
eat	먹다	greet	인사하다
economics	경제학	greeting	인사
education	교육학	half	반
electrical engineering	전기공학	hamburger	햄버거
elementary school	초등학교	have	있다
elementary school student	초등학생	Hawaiʻi	하와이
		here	여기
e-mail	이메일	high school	고등학교
end	끝나다	high school student	고등학생
engagement	약속	history	역사
English	영어	hobby	취미
evening	저녁	home, house	집
every day	날마다	hometown	고향

homework	숙제	lunch	점심
Hong Kong	홍콩	magazine	잡지
horror movie	공포 영화	main character	주인공
hot	덥다	major	전공
hour	시 (counter)	major	전공하다
hour	시간 (duration)	make	만들다
how long/much	얼마	make a telephone call	전화하다
how long/much	얼마나	man	남자
how many, what	몇	many, much	많다
how	어떻게	many, several	여러
how	어떻다	map	지도
I	나*plain*	market	마켓
I	저*hum.*	mechanical	기계 공학
in peace	안녕히	engineering	
in, at	에서	meet	만나다
in, at, on	에	Mexico	멕시코
inside	안	middle, the center	가운데
interesting, fun	재미있다	middle school	중학교
intersection	사거리	middle school student	중학생
I see	네	minute	분 (counter)
item	개 (counter)	Monday	월요일
Japan	일본	money	돈
Japanese style (food)	일식	month	달 (counter)
juice	주스	month	월 (counter)
June	6월(유월)	morning	아침
junior	3학년	mother	어머니
know	알다	movie	영화
Korea	한국	movie theater	극장
Korean language	한국말	much, many	많이
Korean language	한국어	music	음악
Korean style (food)	한식	my	내*plain*
Korea town	한인타운	my	제*hum.*
last, past	지난	name	성함*hon.*
last year	작년	name	이름*plain*
law	법학	narrow	좁다
learn	배우다	nearby, vicinity	근처
left side	왼쪽	neighborhood	동네
lesson, chapter	과	news	뉴스
library	도서관	newspaper	신문
life, living	생활	New York	뉴욕
like	좋아하다	next, following	다음
linguistics	언어학	next year	내년
listen	듣다	night	밤
literature	문학	no	아니요
little	좀	not be (existence)	없다
little	조금	not be (neg. equation)	아니다
live	살다	not know	모르다
Los Angeles (L.A.)	로스앤젤레스	novel	소설
loud(ly)	크게	now	지금

number	번	quiet	조용하다
number	번호	read	읽다
object particle	을/를	reading	독서
of	의	really	정말
often, frequently	자주	really, truly	참
oh	아	receive	받다
oh	어	relationship	사이
okay (OK)	네	repeat after	따라하다
older brother of female	오빠	restaurant	식당
		right side	오른쪽
older brother of male	형	room	방
older sister of female	언니	roommate	룸메이트
older sister of male	누나	run	뛰다
one	하나	Russia	러시아
one	한 (with counter)	Saturday	토요일
only	만	school	학교
open, unfold	펴다	school cafeteria	학교 식당
oral exam	구두 시험	school vacation	방학
other side	건너편	school year	학년
outside	밖	season	계절
over there	저기	see	뵙다 hum.
parents	부모님	see, look	보다 plain
park	공원	sell	팔다
party	파티	semester, academic term	학기
pencil	연필		
people	명 (counter)	senior	4학년
person, people	사람	Seoul	서울
photo, picture	사진	shop	쇼핑하다
physics	물리학	shopping	쇼핑
place, spot	군데 (counter)	short	짧다
play	연극	side, beside	옆
play (tennis)	치다	side, direction	쪽
playground	운동장	sit	앉다
plural particle	들	sleep	자다
poetry	시	slow(ly)	천천히
political science	정치학	so	그렇다
population	인구	so, therefore	그래서
post office	우체국	soccer	축구
practice	연습	sometimes	가끔
practice	연습하다	sophomore	2학년
preparation	준비	sorry	미안하다
prepare	준비하다	sorry	죄송하다
present, gift	선물	spacious, wide	넓다
president	대통령	Spain	스페인
pretty	예쁘다	speak	말하다
probably, perhaps	아마	speech, words	말씀 hon.
engagement	약속	speech, words	말 plain
psychology	심리학	spend time	보내다
question	질문	spring	봄

stamp	우표	thriller	스릴러
station	역	Thursday	목요일
stay	계시다	time	시간
store	가게	to (destination)	에
straight	쭉	today	오늘
straight, upright	똑바로	together	같이
street	길	Tokyo	도쿄
student	학생	tomorrow	내일
student center	학생회관	to not have	없다
study	공부	too much	너무
study	공부하다	topic particle	은/는
subject particle	이/가	top side, above	위
subway	지하철	toward, to	(으)로
subway line	호선	traffic light	신호등
summer	여름	travel	여행
Sunday	일요일	travel	여행하다
supermarket	슈퍼	truck	트럭
swim	수영하다	Tuesday	화요일
swimming	수영	turn	돌다
swimming pool	수영장	two	두 (with counter)
Sydney	시드니	two	둘
take [time]	걸리다	uh	저어
take a course	듣다	umbrella	우산
talk, chat	얘기	uninteresting	재미없다
talk, chat	이야기	Union Building	유니온 빌딩
talk, chat	이야기하다	United Kingdom	영국
tasteless, not tasty	맛없다	United States	미국
teach	가르치다	university	대학교
teacher	선생님	up to (location)	까지
telephone	전화	usually	보통
telephone number	전화 번호	very, really	아주
television	텔레비전	volume	권 (counter)
tennis	테니스	walk	걷다
tennis court	테니스장	warm	따뜻하다
test, exam	시험	we/us/our	우리*plain*
textbook	교과서	we/us/our	저희*hum*
thankful	감사하다	weather	날씨
thankful	고맙다	Wednesday	수요일
that	그	week	주
that (over there)	저	weekend	주말
then	그럼	well	안녕하다
there	거기	well	잘
these days	요즘	Western style (food)	양식
thing	거 (contracted)	what	무엇
thing	것	what	뭐
this	이	what place, where	어디
this	이거	what, what kind of	무슨
this time	이번	when	언제
this year	올해	which	어느

who	누구	write	쓰다
who	누가 (누구+가)	year	년 (counter)
why	왜	yes	네
winter	겨울	yesterday	어제
with	하고	yet, still	아직
woman	여자	you	너
won (Korean currency)	원	younger brother	남동생
		younger sibling	동생
work	일	younger sister	여동생
work	일하다		